CAN TECHNOLOGY INNOVATE TRADITIONAL LEISURE MARKET

JOHN LOK

Made with ♥ on the Notion Press Platform
www.notionpress.com

Contents

Preface

Introduction

Our business society had developed long time from farming period to manufacturing period, then to service industry period, till to nowadays technology service and manufacturing period. It brings this question: Can technology or human behavior may influence economic development? Can technology change traditional leisure market?
Nowadays, on movie and opera art performance lesiure market, our leisures businesses have many different kinds to let consumer individual choice, for example, movie, opera art management, football performance, swimming , bicycle competition performance etc. indoor leisure activities. How can persuade audiences to buy ticket to see any one of these indoor leisure performance? We need to learn audience psychological factor and indoor environment factor if leisure businessmen hope to increase their audience number easily.
On future space city new tourism development market, space cities will not be science fiction, it will be achieved in possible. Whether what benefits it can bring to our future next generation. In this book, I shall explain what is the development differences between smart city development and space city development, then I shall indicate that what challenges to space city development will encounter , next I shall research view points to argue whether space city development is value or not as well as investigate what the actual aims to this space city development. How to learn space city tourism lesiure to let travelers feel more attractive to compare general earth travelling lesiure.

Prologue

Contents

exploring undiscovered adapting
human living planets

Is exploring Mars the most important factor
to influence traveller space travel lesiure choice

The comparison benefit
and risk between space
travel and space exploration

Mars exploration failure factors

Space exploration possible
economic benefits

What is space city tourism

Is Developing space city possible

Developing space city tourism aim

Chapter 6
Computer tool useful leisure Consumer Behavior

- Why China's computer manufacturing and product development industry will be global leader to compete US computer dominant market. p.174-190
    - Factors influence consumers' laptop purchases behavior.
    - Can culture factor influence the computer consumer choice behavior?

Bibliography and further resources

- Computer industry related service market development
- What kinds of technologies innovation products will impact our future lives.
- Autonomous automatic vehicle
- 3 D printer
- Massive open online course education
- Future computer innovative and sustainable food source market

Future computer industry market related business strategy trends

- Government (public) and private partnership property development strategy
- Online Tourism partnership
- Higher education marketing, enrollment,
branding and recruitment strategy

Internet market development trend

- What is Internet entertainment function
- What is Internet learning function
- What is internet for searching information
function
- What is internet for online office
Function
- What is internet for ecommerce
Function

Computer technology related service consumer
negtive emotion factors

- Technology negative influence reasons

Online technology negative influence

- How technology could contribute to bring poor standard
of living to influence our societies

How to avoid to technology brings negative influence on children

- Technology negative influence to low knowledge learner to feel difficult to adopt future new technological labor market
- The negative impact of smartphones/ mobiles and desktop /laptop on human health and life

Avoidance to driving and speaking mobile at the same time

What are the negative effect of electromagnetic waves on human brains from smartphone influence

The laptop and desktop negative influence

CHAPTER ONE

Explaining supply and demand economic theory relationship

The difference between past and nowadays economists their demand and supply economic theory explanation?

The law of supply and demand defines the relationship between the price of a given good or product and the willingness of people to either buy or sell it. Generally, as the price of a good increases, people are willing to supply more and demand less. These economists had explained economic demand and supply theory as below:

Philosopher John Locke is credited with one of the earliest written descriptions of this economic principle in his 1691 publication, Some Considerations of the Consequences of the Lowering of Interest and the Raising of thc Value of Money. Locke addressed the concept of supply and demand as part of a discussion about interest rates in 17th-century England. Many merchants wanted the government to lower the cap on interest rates charged by private lenders so that people could borrow more money and thus purchase more goods. Locke argued that the free-market economy should set rates because government regulation could have unintended consequences. If the lending industry were left alone, interest rates would regulate themselves, Locke wrote: "The price of any commodity rises or falls by the proportion of the number of buyers and sellers."

Sir James Steuart's Inquiry into the Principles of Political Economy, published in 1796, was the first known printed use of the term "supply and demand." When Steuart wrote his treatise on political economy, one of his main concerns was the impact of supply and demand on laborers.

Adam Smith dealt extensively with the topic in his 1776 epic economic work, The Wealth of Nations. Often referred to as the Father of Economics, Smith explained the concept of supply and demand as an "invisible hand" that naturally guides the economy. According to Smith, the invisible hand is the automatic pricing and distribution mechanisms in the economy. Smith described a society in which bakers and butchers provide products that individuals need and want, providing a supply that meets demand and developing an economy that benefits everyone. It is important to note that Smith's ideas haven't gone without critique over the years since his ideas were first published, though. Over time, his ideas have been added to in order to represent the changing times and include concepts such as marginal utility, comparative advantage, entrepreneurship, the time-preference theory of interest, and monetary theory.

One of Marshall's most important contributions to microeconomics was his introduction of the concept of price elasticity of demand, which examines how price changes affect demand. In theory, people buy less of a particular product if the price increases, but Marshall noted that in real life, this behavior was not always true. The prices of some goods can increase without reducing demand, which means their prices are inelastic. Inelastic goods tend to include items such as medication or food that consumers deem crucial to daily life. Marshall argued that supply and demand, costs of production, and price elasticity all work together.

Nowadays economists they explain demand and supply economic theory, they have some different to past economists whose explanation as below:

How Does Supply and Demand Work? The law of supply and demand is a theory that explains the interaction between the sellers of a resource and the buyers of that resource. Generally, as price increases, people are willing to supply more and demand less and vice versa when the price falls.

What does the bottom line mean. Despite the origins of the law of supply and demand beginning hundreds of years ago, it's still a topic frequently referenced and utilized today in economic theory and discussions. The theory has developed over time to accommodate recent technological and economical advancements, but the basic ideas of the theory remain largely the same.

Does demand depend on supply?

Supply and Demand Determine the Price of Goods and Quantities Produced and Consumed. Consumers may exhaust the available supply of a good by purchasing a given good or service at a high volume. This leads to an increase in demand. As demand increases, the available supply also decreases.

What does market demand depend on?

Market factors affecting demand of consumer goods. The demand for a good increases or decreases depending on several factors. This includes the product's price, perceived quality, advertising spend, consumer income, consumer confidence, and changes in taste and fashion.

Who controls the demand in supply and demand?

Supply and demand are in turn determined by technology and the conditions under which people operate. At one extreme, the market could be populated by a large number of virtually identical sellers and buyers (for example, the market for ballpoint pens).

What are the two laws of demand and supply?

The law of demand holds that the demand level for a product or a resource will decline as its price rises, and rise as the price drops. Conversely, the law of supply says higher prices boost supply of an economic good while lower ones tend to diminish it.

What factors affect demand and supply?

Price fluctuations are a strong factor affecting supply and demand. When a product gets expensive enough that the average consumer no longer feels it is worth it to buy the product, then the demand declines. This leads to cuts in production that will hopefully stabilize the product's value.

What factors affect demand and demand?

Demand may be defined as the quantity of a commodity that a consumer is able and willing to buy, at each possible price, over a given period of time. • Essential elements of demand are quantity, ability, willingness, prices, and period of time.

Which factors affect supply?

Generally, the supply of a product depends on its price and other variables such as the cost of production.

a. Price. Price can be understood as what the consumer is willing to pay to receive a good or service. ...

b. Cost of production. ...

c. Technology. ...

d. Governments' policies. ...

e. Transportation condition.

How does supply and demand work together?

It's a fundamental economic principle that when supply exceeds demand for a good or service, prices fall. When demand exceeds supply, prices tend to rise. There is an inverse relationship between the supply and prices of goods and services when demand is unchanged.

What happens to supply when demand increases?

An increase in demand, all other things unchanged, will cause the equilibrium price to rise; quantity supplied will increase. A decrease in demand will cause the equilibrium price to fall; quantity supplied will decrease.

What is the theory of demand?

Demand theory describes the way that changes in the quantity of a good or service demanded by consumers affects its price in the market, The theory states that the higher the price of a product is, all else equal, the less of it will be demanded, inferring a downward sloping demand curve.

What are the 4 basic laws of supply and demand?

1) If the supply increases and demand stays the same, the price will go down. 2) If the supply decreases and demand stays the same, the price will go up. 3) If the supply stays the same and demand increases, the price will go up. 4) If the supply stays the same and demand decreases, the price will go down.

The different types of demand are as follows:

i. Individual and Market Demand: ...

ii. Organization and Industry Demand: ...

iii. Autonomous and Derived Demand: ...

iv. Demand for Perishable and Durable Goods: ...

v. Short-term and Long-term Demand:

What creates demand for a product?

You can create demand for a unique product if you can manage to solve a persistent problem for the consumer. People are always running away from pain, and providing them with an outlet is a sure-fire way to create massive demand for your goods.

What are the 7 factors that affect supply?

The seven factors which affect the changes of supply are as follows: (i) Natural Conditions (ii) Technical Progress (iii) Change in Factor Prices (iv) Transport Improvements (v) Calamities (vi) Monopolies (vii) Fiscal Policy.

What can affect demand?

Factors Affecting Demand

Price of the Product. ...

The Consumer's Income. ...

The Price of Related Goods. ...
The Tastes and Preferences of Consumers. ...
The Consumer's Expectations. ...
The Number of Consumers in the Market.
What are the three factors affecting demand?
The demand for a product will be influenced by several factors:

Price. Usually viewed as the most important factor that affects demand. ...

Income levels. ...
Consumer tastes and preferences. ...
Competition. ...
Fashions.
What are the 4 factors of supply?
The four factors that can shift the supply curve include natural conditions, input prices, technology, and government.
What causes increase in supply?
If the cost of production is lower, the profits available at a given price will increase, and producers will produce more. With more produced at every price, the supply curve will shift to the right, meaning an increase in supply.
What causes supply changes?
A change in supply is an economic term that describes when the suppliers of a given good or service alter production or output. A change in supply can occur as a result of new technologies, such as more efficient or less expensive production processes, or a change in the number of competitors in the market.
Is supply and demand a good strategy?

When it comes to profit placement, supply and demand zones can be a great tool as well. Always place your profit target ahead of a zone so that you don't risk giving back all your profits when the open interest in that zone is filled.

How is demand created?
Demand creation is a process that fuels the revenue pipeline so the sales team can meet or exceed their quotas. In other words, it takes your big idea — the creative appeal of your brand — and turns it into sales. That sounds a lot like demand generation, which often gets confused with lead generation.
What are the two parts of demand?
Economists define demand as the quantity of a good or service that buyers are willing and able to buy at all possible prices during a certain time period.

Notice that there are two components to demand: willingness to purchase and ability to pay.

Can we control demand?

If you're willing to think and act strategically, you can easily manipulate the laws of supply and demand. It should be surprising to learn, however, that by manipulating the laws of supply and demand, you can make more profit in less time and with far fewer headaches

How do you control demand?

Here are five short-term actions to improve your demand variability management plans in this time of uncertainty:

Maintain transparent, proactive relationships with your suppliers. ...

Activate alternate sources of supply. ...

Reduce lead times. ...

Update inventory policy and planning. ...

Align supply and demand management.

What are the 8 types of demand?

There are 8 states of demand: negative demand, no demand, latent demand, falling demand, irregular demand, full demand, overfull demand and unwholesome demand.

What is Demand?

Types of Determinants of Demand. Every factor has a unique impact on demand. ...

Price of the Product. ...

The Income of the Consumers. ...

Number of Buyers in the Market. ...

Consumer's Expectations. ...

Tastes and Preferences of The Consumers. ...

Complement Goods. ...

Substitute Product.

What is theory of supply?

The law of supply is a fundamental principle of economic theory which states that, keeping other factors constant, an increase in price results in an increase in quantity supplied. In other words, there is a direct relationship between price and quantity: quantities respond in the same direction as price changes.

What are the types of supply?

There are five types of supply—market supply, short-term supply, long-term supply, joint supply, and composite supply.

Which comes first supply or demand?
Demand comes first and it's followed by the corresponding supplies. Supply and demand are both very important to economic activity. Supply is the total amount of a particular good or service available at a given time to consumers at a given price. Demand is a representation of a consumer's desire to purchase goods and services; it acts as a measurement of a consumer's willingness to purchase a specific good or service at a given price. These two economic forces influence each other; they are both important for the economy because they impact the prices of consumer goods and services within an economy and the quantities produced and consumed. Supply and demand are both keys to understanding the economy because they reflect the prices and quantities of consumer goods and services within an economy.

What are the relationship between demand and supply?
According to market economy theory, the relationship between supply and demand balances out at a point in the future; this point is called the equilibrium price.
Economists and companies analyze the relationship between supply and demand when making strategic product decisions. Both economists and companies analyze the relationship between supply and demand when making strategic product decisions. The assumption behind a market economy is that supply and demand are the best determinants for an economy's growth and health.
Consumer Behavior Influences Demand
One way that companies or economists might analyze this relationship is to create graphs that chart the equilibrium price of certain goods and services in order to determine product development and their production schedule. Consumer behavior dictates which products are produced and sold because consumers create the demand that companies attempt to meet. As a result, companies may study consumer behavior in an attempt to understand the current demand and predict future demand. It is vital that companies maintain the capacity to produce enough of a good or service that they can satisfy consumer demands.
Supply and demand are two sides of the same market coin. Generally, supply is how much of something is available or will be produced at a certain price. Demand is how much of something people want to purchase or consume at a certain price. One way to develop a more precise

relationship between the two is to consider how the price of something affects its supply and its demand. Generally when the price of a good goes up, so does the supply, since firms are willing to create more when they can sell at higher prices. But when the price of a good goes up consumers will, at the same time, generally demand less. It is the interaction of supply and demand that determines how much will be produced and consumed and at what price, converging to a state known as equilibrium.

CHAPTER TWO

Human social job change demand and supply relationship

The relationship between social change and human behavior

Human Behavioral network job brings social economic benefits

Whether human social job change it depends on social job demand more or job supply more? What does human network job mean ? Why may human network job be popular? Why human network job behavior may influence economy ?

Nowadays internet is popular to use. We can apply internet to find data , search any new things, even earn money. Why does internet may become huma network job source. For example, e-publish may be one kind of new human network job. Any authors may apply internet channel to help them to sell electronic or paper books from e-publisher web store. They may apply facebook, you tub etc. any online channel to promote themselves new books to let new readers to know whether when they may buy themselves favourable new topic books to read from electronic publisher web store.

Thus, future electronic publisher industry may help any authors to build internet network platform to help them to sell and promote ot advertise their any one new electronic or paper book topic to let global any one reader to choose to buy their any new topic books from electronic publisher web store easily and conveniently. However, it implies that electronic network platform author may be one kind of future new human network job in our societies.

How electronic network platform author job may bring economy benefit in macro economy view? A person can have few friends, contacts and still be very influential if these few
friends and contacts are themselves highly influential, e.g. one author must not need to know any one reader in global society. When they like to choose any electronic books from electronic internet network platform. They may become the author's any one topic book buyer, when they feel the author's any one topic book is fun and attract they make decision to buth the strange author whose the topic book from electronic book publisher's platform web store conventiently in short time. Although, they are strangers, they do not know themselves , but the reader can understand what it way that made Google from writing platofrm to create new creative mind and typing network job method to replace traditional hand writing book method for global authors. It will be one kind of new human network writing job.

Hence, global any one reader can apply an innovative search engine , such as google.com to find whether whom author personal new topic books are value to read from internet.
Then, the electroniuc publisher's web store may be new book store platform sale network to help the author to sell many electronic or paper books from electronic network platform
in short time. So, internet may be future new network plaform to help global any one author to create network writing job absolutely. Furthermore, internet may be popular social media
to help any one author to build goold relationship between his/her readers. It is one kind of new network, human network job. New authors do not need to buy many paper books to prepare to put in any one book shop warehouse. Their every book can print on demand to reduce out of book stock in any one book shop. They may choose to sell either electronic books or paper books both from any one book publisher web store. So, electronic network platform may be one kind of good writing channel to help human authors to create income and it can also help authors to bring new creative mind and new topic fun content books to let readers to know and buy to read from electronic publisher network platform.

Why does human behavior may be one kind of new human network job to bring global economic advantages. ALthough, it may be free income or without inocme, but the person does the network behavior, his/her behavior may be bring advantages to influence many other people's health. For this case, when a worker in a coffee shop in an airport gets a vaccination aganinst the flu, it does not only helps him or her stay healthy, but also helps the many travellers who might otherwise have been inflected if that workers caught the flu. So, the externality , the result implies the vaccination of even a part of a community conveys benefits to the whole community. For example, governments pay special attention to the vaccinations of school children, teachers, health mothers, and the elderly, categories of people particularly susceptible not only to catching, but also to transmitting a disease.

It is not accidential that governments are heavily involved with vaccination . When there are externalities, free market, fail to persuade individual incentives with society's
their the worker's decision of whether to get a vaccine ends up attracting whether other people get sick. The workers might not fully take all these other people's potential suffering into account when making her or his vaccination decision.

As Stanford University does many suggestions, understand this and tries to help them make the right decisions and so providers free flu vaccines for its staff and students.

Small pockets of unvaccinated individuals can allow a disease to gain a spread more widely well-being. For example, parent weighing the costs and benefits of a vaccine for their child is not always thinking of the consequences of that vaccination to other people. THese are markets in which subsidizing or regulating behavior can make everyone better off. Because the reason for requiring that a child be vaccinated before enrolling in school is not just to protect that child, because each child's vaccination affects others via potential contagions.

On conclusion, it seems that many traditional paper book publish business begain to change to electronic book publish business. Due, to online technology existence, it influences many readers choose to buy electronic books to read. Hence, due to readers reading demand change which is from paper book reading habit to electonic book reading habit.Then,it explains that electornic book supply number depends on electronic book reader reading demand in economic view.

Robots take our jobs behavioral and economy influences

Robot job behavior brings economy influences

Whether robot labor needs are depended on employer labor demand more or robot labor number supply more? If one day robots can replace human to do simple, even complex jobs. They will bring what influences to our global societial economy.The popular economic refrain declares that the global middle class is dying and robots will soon take our jobs, e.g. shopping center customer service jobs, library service jobs, cinema ticket sale jobs, restaurant kitchen cooker jobs, even, bus drivers, taxi drivers etc. public transport driving jobs, accountant, doctors etc. professional jobs. Whether it is beautiful or petty matter if our future societies have many human jobs can be replaced to do from robots. Businessman must may reduce to employ employees and reduce to pay salary or wage, when robots can be replaced to do their employees tasks. But, societies must bring unemployement rate rises , due to societies will have many people loss jobs when their employers choose to buy robots to serve their clients or do any office tasks or customer service or cleaning etc. tasks.

In micro economy view, employers may save money in long term, but in macro economy view, it will cause unemployment ratio rises , even crime rate rises when there are many people lose jobs in societies. These models of doom, though, fail to account for the hundreds of businesses riding the waves of change in their industries when robots may be invented to replace human to do many simple , even complex tasks in our future societies.

WE may image that one small factory needs to manufacture fishes canes to sell to supermarket, the small , cheaper stuff and higher margin parts of the fishes manufacture industry. Before, this factory needs to employe many human factory workers need to help every fresh customer makeing the perfect fishing gear, designed for performance, durability, and cost in order to achieve to manufacture every fish cane in whole fished processing manufacturing stages. Every worker needs to spend about 15 to twenty minutes to finish every fish cane , till to delivery to any supermarket to sell. If this fish canes manufacturing factory can apply manufacturing robots to help them to finish any one working tasks , every robot can only spend five minutes to finish whole fresh fish cane manufacturing process. Thus, every robot can help this factory save 10 to 15 minutes time to finsh every fish cane

manufacturing process. IN fact, time is money, because when every robot can help this factory to reduce 10 to 15 minutes time to compare human worker. Then, this factory can finish about 20 fish canes in one hour if it can use robot to help it to manufacture fish canes. Otherwise, if this factory still use human workers to help it to manufacture fish canes, then it can finsh about 3 to 4 fish canes in one hour. SO, the manufacturing efficiency ensures that robots must help this fish manufacturing factory to raise fish canes number more than human workers. So, in robotic behavioral economy view, manufacturing robots must help this fish canes manufacturing factory to raise fish canes manufacturing number and deliver increasing number to supermarkets to prepare to sell every day. Robots can help this fish canes manufacturing factory bring manufacturing time saving, rising manufacturing efficiency, improving performance and reducing wages expenditure long time advantages in micro economy view. However, manufacturing robots can also bring disadvanages to society, e.g. increasing unemployment ratio, increasing crime rate,
this factory workers will lose jobs and income, they need earn social welfare from government and increasing government finance pressure in short time, even long time in macro economic view.

Stanford University graduate program in economics, Scott lecturer explained that "in demand and supply economic theory for robots supply and demand case, robots supply number increasing may influence human workers demand number decrease. It sometimes calls " the efficient frontier".

No specific human beings were mentioned in any of economics classes. As robots supply and demand in market case, They (robots) may be purely theoretical " agents" who reached to the most reasonable sale prices in order to persuade any one businessman buyer to make manufacturing robot buying decision whether robots can help him / her to bring how much saving time , saving money, saving cost, improving performance, efficiency economic benefit before he/she plans to reduce workers number when he/ she decides to apply robots to replace human workers in his/her factory or office or any service department, e.g. cinema ticket sale service, shopping center customer service, shopping center cleaning , supermarket customer service etc. service or sale tasks. When robots can replace human to do any one of these tasks in any organizations. So, robots may be human worker agents who reached to prices the way robots would react to a software command. There was nothing that explained why some people thrived and others did n't or why truly brilliant, hardworking people could fail when much lazier folks succeeded." Having been admitted to the Stanford University graduate program in economics, Scott lecturer hoped to get his answers there.

How robots influence our future social changing? Using the right technology can be a boon to your business in this economy. For internet example, it is easier than ever to find well-matched customers all around the world, to stay in contact with them, and to more quickly design the products they want. If you focus solely on being cutting -edge, though you risk letting the technology

take over what should be very robust relationships with your customers , employees, and colleagues. IN nowaddays society, technoligical advances and cutomation, personal

relationships in business are more crucial than ever. I mean that robots can not replace human to serve clients to let them to feel more comfortable and passion more easily. For shoe shop case example, if the shoe shop apply one robot to serve its clients to replace human shoe salesperson to serve its shoe customers. Robots ensure that they can not persuade every shoe potential buyer to make shoe buying decision more easily when robots need to contact every shoe potential buyer. The reason is simple, because robots can not touch any one shoe buyer individual emotion very easier.

If the shoe buyer needs the robots to help him/her to choose any right shoe styles when he/she can not feel himself / herself can make the most right shoe style choice decision. The robots can not replace human shoe salesperson to make shoe style choice judgement more easily. They must need longer time to analyze whether which shoe style may be the most suitable to the shoe buyer. Otherwise, human shoe salesperson may attempt to make the most right shoe style choice decision to help any one shoe buyer to chooce the most right style shoe because he/she owns shoe style sale experience, shoe style knowledge, the most important reason is that they can feel every shoe customer individual emotion to touch whether he/she will feel comfortable or happy when they attempt to help every shoe customer to seek the most right shoe style in every shoe customer whole shoe searching processing. Othwerwise, serving robots are only one machine, they can not touch or feel every shoe customer individual emotion whether he/she feel comfortable or unhappy or happy when they need to contact them in whole shoe searching processing. Hence, I believe that some tasks robots can

not repalce human staff to do very easily. Otherwise, robots may bring disadvanatges to let any one businessman to loss his/her customers, due to robots can not touch every customer
emotion to compare human staff in service tasks more easily. Robots serving customer behaviors may cause money lose and customers number lose to the shop in micro economic view.

On conclusion, in demand and supply economic theory for robots supply and demand case, robots supply number increasing may influence human workers demand number decrease. So, it seems that robots number supply will be depended on global robots supply number more than robots demand number because when human began to accept robots to replace human to do general simple jobs in global labor market. Then, it means that global robots labor number must need to be increased in order to satisfy global businessmen workers number need. If any kinds of robot workers manufacture number is not enough to be supplied to let global future businessmen to buy, then robot supply will be shortage and they can not provide to satisfy global businessmen robots labour purchase need. So, future robot number will be depended on supply more than demand.

CHAPTER THREE

Human intellectual demand and supply behavior relationship

Intellectual human economic behaviors

What does intellectual human economic behaviors mean ? Human foolish behavior is depended on social enjoyment need more or material social supply more? I believe that when we choose or decide to do intellectual behaviors, then our societies will be influenced to bring economic growth in consequence.I shall attempt to indicate pollution case to explain how and why eithet our intellectual or foolish behaviors may bring economic growth or recession in consequence as below:

On one hand, for air pollution social case aspect example, if we only consider to buy cars to drive for working aim or holiday leisure aim. Then, our societies air will be polluted. Our health will be influenced to bad. Our car driving behaviors may cause global environment air pollution serously. In long tiem, global air pollution will bring our bodies health to be bad. Although, ourselves car driving behaviors may bring our driving travelling leisure enjoyment and comfortable feeling in short time, also we so not need to pay public transport fare often, but we need to compensate ourselves health economic intangible loss due to air pollution , when cars number increases, dirty air will cause ouselves health to become bad.

In the result, we will need to pay more medical expenditure when we are old age, due to ourselves bodies will become bad, due to we breathe global dirty air every day, due to ourselves cars pollute air in long time, e.g. 10 to 20 years, even 30 more without limited air pollution environment. So, driving cars behavior may be one kind of human foolish behavior and our foolish behavior may bring ourselves future long time medical expenditure absolutely.

One the other hand, water pollution social aspect, if we often keep much rubblish to pollute sea, oil exploration porcessing pollute ocean , ships gas pollute ocaen, then fishes will eat polluted food and drive dirty water, due to global ocean is polluted.

In fact, because human only to conside how to buy boats to carry on leisure enjoyment activities, or catch cruises to travel on the sea. Also, oil manufacturers only consider researching anywhere to find new oil exploration places to manufacture oil product, when their oil exploration processes pollute ocarn . Consequently, global fishes drink polluted warer or eat polluted food. They will have poison. SO, human will have high chance to eat poison polluted fishes, due to fishes are poison or are polluted. So, human is doing foolish activities, we only hope to find oil exploration places to pollute ocean or we only spend money to buy ticket to catch ships to travel anywhere in global ocean. All of these human foolish behaviors will bring pollution to global ocean. On consequently, we will need to compensate to eat polluted or dirty or poision fishes, ourselves bodies health will be bad. In long time, we need have high chance to pay medical expenditure when we are old. So, pollution case may be one good example to explain how and why human foolish behavior may influence ourselves future need to compensate serious medical loss.

All of these human foolish behavior will bring pollution to global ocean. On consequently, we will need to compensate to eat polluted or dirty or poison fishcd , ourselves bodies health will be bad. In long time, we will have high chance to pay medical expenditure, when we are old. So, pollution case may be one good example to explain how and why human ourselves intellectual or foolish behaviors may influence future long time economic loss or economic growth or recession in micro and micro economic view.

On another water pollution aspect hand, if we often keep rubbish to sea, oil exploration processing pollutes ocean and ships' gas pollute ocean, then fishes will eat polluted food and drink dirty water, due to fishes will eat polluted food and drink dirty sea water because the global ocean is polluted seriously.

In fact, because human only consider how to buy boats to carry on any leisure water activities, or catches cruises to travel on the sea. Also, oil manufacturers only consider any where to find oil exploratin places to manufacture oil products from ocean, when their pol exploration processes can plooute ocean. Consequently, global fishes drink polluted water or eat direty food. They will have poison. So, human will have high chance to eat poison fishes.

Otherwise, such as pollutin case, it can infuence inflation or deflation. Consequently, the reason indicates supply and demand theory. If air pollution is serious, then we will consider health issue, global cars demand number may be influenced to reduce, when global cars number demand will reduce, global car prices and supply number will need to change to fall down in order to attract or persuade global car consumers choose to make car purchase decision.

Hence, global car manufacture number and car price will be influenced to reduce, due to global air pollution issue. Consequently, deflation will occur because when the country citizen usually does not spend much extra saving money to buy car expensive goods. Money value will be low. Otherwise, if global cair pollution is not serious, human considers to buy cars to enjoy driving leisure lives. So, global car demand is influenced to increase , also global car price will also influenced to increase.

Consequently, gobal human will choose to buy cars to drive. Due to we accept to spend extra saving to buy expensive car goods. Car sale price and supply may be influenced to rise up. Money value is influenced to reduce. Inflation may be influenced, due to global car consumers number increases, we would not have extra money to spend easily. Car expensive goods expenditure influences our spending habit to avoid to make car purchase decision more easily. So, human intellectual or foolish activities may bring inflation or deflation consequency in possible indirectly in macro economic view.

On conclusion, above pollution case explain that how and why human intellectual or foolish economic behaviors may bring inflation or deflation consequency as wll as economic growth or recession consequency as well as any goods demand and supply increasing or decreasing consequency. It implies that human behavior may have indirect relationship to influence any goods demand and supply number to either increase or decrease result as well as any goods price will be influenced to increase or decrease in micro and macro economic view. Hence, Human foolish behavior is depended on social enjoyment need more or material social supply more because human needs to raise enjoyment feel , so we will choose to do foolish behavior, e.g. air pollution, when many people choose to buy cars to drive to replace catch public transport. So, such as car market, it depends on car demand number more than car supply number absolutely in demand and supply view.

The relationship between social change and human behavior

Why does economic changes may influence human individual behavioral change? I shall attempt to indicate shopping behavior and staying at home behavior to explain their case and effect relationsip as below:
Human behavior can be influenced by economic change or economic change can be influenced by human behavior? Why does recession may influence consumers reduce shopping desire? In social recession suitation, it is possible that many people lose jobs suddenly, due to businessmen lose many customers. They need to make decision to reduce employees number in order to continue to keep businesses. Consequently, many firms (organizations) their employees may lose jobs. When they have much time, due to lose jobs, they will feel to avoid to spend too much time and money to go to shopping often. Many losing jobs people, they will often stay at homes. So, they will reduce time to go to shopping, then non essential products won't their preferable choice purchase products. Hence, recession will change many losing jobs people their shopping or consumption desires to avoid to buy non essential products often . Usually when economic boom, many people have jobs to do because consumers number must increase when many people have jobs to do. Then, many people can accept to spend money to buy non essential products often. Many people feel spend time to go to shopping can satisfy their purchase of any kinds of new products useful psychology or desire. So, recession is one good example to explain it can influence many people do not like often to leave homes to go to shopping easily. Many people like to stay at homes, becaue they feel worry about spending too much shopping time when they leave homes. Their staying home time is one good negative shopping behavior example. So, economic change may influence human individual behavior changes , they have direct cause and efect relationship in behavioral economic view.
May human behavior influence economic change? Is it possible that human behavior may bring the country social economic change in macro economic or micro behavioral economic view ? I shall indicate publishing industry example. Do you feel that if there are many students feel learning is very important when they read many books or many of students feel interesting to read or they have reading new books in habit, then it is possible that the country will have many students like to spend time to go to any book shops to choose the books, they feel that they can help they learn new knowledge.

Then the country will increase students number, they often spend time to visit any one book shop every week. Their visiting book shops behavior which may become their habits. So, the country will increase students number, they often spend time to visit book shops. Also, it implies that visiting book shops behaviors may be their behavioral habits.

So, when the country has many students often spend time to visit book shops , their visiting book shops behaviors may help any one book shop to raise books sale chance. So, the country's student individual often visiting book shop behaviors, their habitual visiting book shops behaviors must may assist help any one book shop to increase books sale number absolutely.

Consequently, any one book shop , its books sale bumber must be influenced to increase to increase because the country will have many students like or feel need visit book shops habit in order to choose any suitable books to buy to read at home in order to raise themselves learning effort. When the country has many bok shops often have many students visit their book shops, then their books sale number may be influenced to increase. It explain why student individual visiting book shop behavior may help any one book shop sale number increases also. So, visiting shops products sale number is depended on online products supply number, if online products supply number increases, then it may cause many customers choose to buy the kind of products from online webstore. So, any shop products sale number will depend on onlint products supply number in supply and demand view.

CHAPTER FOUR

Technology or human behavior whether may influence economic growth or recession

Human Behavioral network job brings social economic benefits

What does human network job mean ? Why may human network job be popular? Why human network job behavior may influence economy ? Nowadays internet is popular to use. We can apply internet to find data , search any new things, even earn money. Why does internet may become huma network job source. For example, e-publish may be one kind of new human network job. Any authors may apply internet channel to help them to sell electronic or paper books from e-publisher web store. They may apply facebook, you tub etc. any online channel to promote themselves new books to let new readers to know whether when they may buy themselves favourable new topic books to read from electronic publisher web store.

Thus, future electronic publisher industry may help any authors to build internet network platform to help them to sell and promote ot advertise their any one new electronic or paper book topic to let global any one reader to choose to buy their any new topic books from electronic publisher web store easily and conveniently. However, it implies that electronic network platform author may be one kind of future new human network job in our societies.

How electronic network platform author job may bring economy benefit in macro economy view? A person can have few friends, contacts and still be very influential if these few
friends and contacts are themselves highly influential, e.g. one author must not need to know any one reader in global society. When they like to choose any electronic books from electronic internet network platform. They may become the author's any one topic book buyer, when they feel the author's any one topic book is fun and attract they make decision to buth the strange author whose the topic book from electronic book publisher's platform web store conventiently in short time. Although, they are strangers, they do not know themselves , but the reader can understand what it way that made Google from writing platofrm to create new creative mind and typing network job method to replace traditional hand writing book method for global authors. It will be one kind of new human network writing job.

Hence, global any one reader can apply an innovative search engine , such as google.com to find whether whom author personal new topic books are value to read from internet.
Then, the electroniuc publisher's web store may be new book store platform sale network to help the author to sell many electronic or paper books from electronic network platform
in short time. So, internet may be future new network plaform to help global any one author to create network writing job absolutely. Furthermore, internet may be popular social media
to help any one author to build goold relationship between his/her readers. It is one kind of new network, human network job. New authors do not need to buy many paper books to prepare to put in any one book shop warehouse. Their every book can print on demand to reduce out of book stock in any one book shop. They may choose to sell either electronic books or paper books both from any one book publisher web store. So, electronic network platform may be one kind of good writing channel to help human authors to create income and it can also help authors to bring new creative mind and new topic fun content books to let readers to know and buy to read from electronic publisher network platform.

Why does human behavior may be one kind of new human network job to bring global economic advantages. ALthough, it may be free income or without inocme, but the person does the network behavior, his/her behavior may be bring advantages to influence many other people's health. For this case, when a worker in a coffee shop in an airport gets a vaccination aganinst the flu, it does not only helps him or her stay healthy, but also helps the many travellers who might otherwise have been inflected if that workers caught the flu. So, the externality , the result implies the vaccination of even a part of a community conveys benefits to the whole community. For example, governments pay special attention to the vaccinations of school children, teachers, health mothers, and the elderly, categories of people particularly susceptible not only to catching, but also to transmitting a disease.

It is not accidential that governments are heavily involved with vaccination . When there are externalities, free market, fail to persuade individual incentives with society's

their the worker's decision of whether to get a vaccine ends up attracting whether other people get sick. The workers might not fully take all these other people's potential suffering into account when making her or his vaccination decision.

As Stanford University does many suggestions, understand this and tries to help them make the right decisions and so providers free flu vaccines for its staff and students.

Small pockets of unvaccinated individuals can allow a disease to gain a spread more widely well-being. For example, parent weighing the costs and benefits of a vaccine for their child is not always thinking of the consequences of that vaccination to other people. THese are markets in which subsidizing or regulating behavior can make everyone better off. Because the reason for requiring that a child be vaccinated before enrolling in school is not just to protect that child, because each child's vaccination affects others via potential contagions.

Robots take our jobs behavioral and economy influences

Robot job behavior brings economy influences

If one day robots can replace human to do simple, even complex jobs. They will bring what influences to our global societial economy.The popular economic refrain declares that the

global middle class is dying and robots will soon take our jobs, e.g. shopping center customer service jobs, library service jobs, cinema ticket sale jobs, restaurant kitchen cooker jobs,

even, bus drivers, taxi drivers etc. public transport driving jobs, accountant, doctors etc. professional jobs. Whether it is beautiful or petty matter if our future societies have many human jobs can be replaced to do from robots.

Businessman must may reduce to employ employees and reduce to pay salary or wage, when robots can be replaced to do their employees tasks. But, societies must bring unemployement rate rises , due to societies will have many people loss jobs when their employers choose to buy robots to serve their clients or do any office tasks or customer service or cleaning etc. tasks.

In micro economy view, employers may save money in long term, but in macro economy view, it will cause unemployment ratio rises , even crime rate rises when there are many people lose
jobs in societies. These models of doom, though, fail to account for the hundreds of businesses riding the waves of change in their industries when robots may be invented to replace human to do many simple , even complex tasks in our future societies.

WE may image that one small factory needs to manufacture fishes canes to sell to supermarket, the small , cheaper stuff and higher margin parts of the fishes manufacture industry. Before, this factory needs to employe many human factory workers need to help every fresh customer makeing the perfect fishing gear, designed for performance, durability, and cost in order to achieve to manufacture every fish cane in whole fished processing manufacturing stages. Every worker needs to spend about 15 to twenty minutes to finish every fish cane , till to delivery to any supermarket to sell. If this fish canes manufacturing factory can apply manufacturing robots to help them to finish any one working tasks , every robot can only spend five minutes to finish whole fresh fish cane manufacturing process. Thus, every robot can
help this factory save 10 to 15 minutes time to finsh every fish cane manufacturing process. IN fact, time is money, because when every robot can help this factory to reduce 10 to 15 minutes time to compare human worker. Then, this factory can finish about 20 fish canes in one hour if it can use robot to help it to manufacture fish canes. Otherwise, if this factory still use human workers to help it to manufacture fish canes, then it can finsh about 3 to 4 fish canes in one hour. SO, the manufacturing efficiency ensures that robots must help this fish manufacturing factory to raise fish canes number more than human workers. So, in robotic behavioral economy view, manufacturing robots must help this fish canes manufacturing factory to raise fish canes manufacturing number and deliver increasing number to supermarkets to prepare to sell every day. Robots can help this fish canes manufacturing factory bring manufacturing time saving,

rising manufacturing efficiency, improving performance and reducing wages expenditure long time advantages in micro economy view. However, manufacturing robots can also bring disadvanages to society, e.g. increasing unemployment ratio, increasing crime rate,
this factory workers will lose jobs and income, they need earn social welfare from government and increasing government finance pressure in short time, even long time in macro economic view.

Stanford University graduate program in economics, Scott lecturer explained that "in demand and supply economic theory for robots supply and demand case, robots supply number increasing may influence human workers demand number decrease. It sometimes calls " the efficient frontier".
No specific human beings were mentioned in any of economics classes. As robots supply and demand in market case, They (robots) may be purely theoretical " agents" who reached to the most reasonable sale prices in order to persuade any one businessman buyer to make manufacturing robot buying decision whether robots can help him / her to bring how much saving time , saving money, saving cost, improving performance, efficiency economic benefit before he/she plans to reduce workers number when he/she decides to apply robots to replace human workers in his/her factory or office or any service department, e.g. cinema ticket sale service, shopping center customer service, shopping center cleaning , supermarket customer service etc. service or sale tasks. When robots can replace human to do any one of these tasks in any organizations. So, robots may be human worker agents who reached to prices the way robots would react to a software
command. There was nothing that explained why some people thrived and others did n't or why truly brilliant, hardworking people could fail when much lazier folks succeeded." Having been admitted to the Stanford University graduate program in economics, Scott lecturer hoped to get his answers there.

How robots influence our future social changing? Using the right technology can be a boon to your business in this economy. For internet example, it is easier than ever to find well-matched customers all around the world, to stay in contact with them, and to more quickly design the products they want. If you focus solely on being cutting -edge, though you risk letting the technology
take over what should be very robust relationships with your customers , employees, and colleagues. IN nowaddays society, technoligical advances

and cutomation, personal

relationships in business are more crucial than ever. I mean that robots can not replace human to serve clients to let them to feel more comfortable and passion more easily. For shoe shop case example, if the shoe shop apply one robot to serve its clients to replace human shoe salesperson to serve its shoe customers. Robots ensure that they can not persuade every shoe potential buyer to make shoe buying decision more easily when robots need to contact every shoe potential buyer. The reason is simple, because robots can not touch any one shoe buyer individual emotion very easier.

If the shoe buyer needs the robots to help him/her to choose any right shoe styles when he/she can not feel himself / herself can make the most right shoe style choice decision. The robots can not replace human shoe salesperson to make shoe style choice judgement more easily. They must need longer time to analyze whether which shoe style may be the most suitable to the shoe buyer. Otherwise, human shoe salesperson may attempt to make the most right shoe style choice decision to help any one shoe buyer to chooce the most right style shoe because he/she owns shoe style sale experience, shoe style knowledge, the most important reason is that they can feel every shoe customer individual emotion to touch whether he/she will feel comfortable or happy when they attempt to help every shoe customer to seek the most right shoe style in every shoe customer whole shoe searching processing. Othwerwise, serving robots are only one machine, they can not touch or feel every shoe customer individual emotion whether he/she feel comfortable or unhappy or happy when they need to contact them in whole shoe searching processing. Hence, I believe that some tasks robots can

not repalce human staff to do very easily. Otherwise, robots may bring disadvanatges to let any one businessman to loss his/her customers, due to robots can not touch every customer

emotion to compare human staff in service tasks more easily. Robots serving customer behaviors may cause money lose and customers number lose to the shop in micro economic view.

Intellectual human economic behaviors

What does intellectual human economic behaviors mean ? I believe that when we choose or decide to do intellectual behaviors, then our societies will be influenced to bring economic growth in consequence.I shall attempt to indicate pollution case to explain how and why eithet our intellectual or foolish behaviors may bring economic growth or recession in consequence

as below:
On one hand, for air pollution social case aspect example, if we only consider to buy cars to drive for working aimr or holiday leisure aim. Then, our societies air will be polluted. Our health will be influenced to bad. Our car driving behaviors may cause global environment air pollution serously. In long tiem, global air pollution will bring our bodies health to be bad. Although, ourselves car driving behaviors may bring our driving travelling leisure enjoyment and comfortable feeling in short time, also we so not need to pay public transport fare often, but we need to compensate ourselves health economic intangible loss due to air pollution , when cars number increases, dirty air will cause ouselves health to become bad.
In the result, we will need to pay more medical expenditure when we are old age, due to ourselves bodies will become bad, due to we breathe global dirty air every day, due to ourselves cars pollute air in long time, e.g. 10 to 20 years, even 30 more without limited air pollution environment. So, driving cars behavior may be one kind of human foolish behavior and our foolish behavior may bring ourselves future long time medical expenditure absolutely.
One the other hand, water pollution social aspect, if we often keep much rubblish to pollute sea, oil exploration porcessing pollute ocean , ships gas pollute ocaen, then fishes will eat polluted food and drive dirty water, due to global ocean is polluted.
In fact, because human only to conside how to buy boats to carry on leisure enjoyment activities, or catch cruises to travel on the sea. Also, oil manufacturers only consider researching anywhere to find new oil exploration placcs to manufacture oil product, when their oil exploration processes pollute ocarn . Consequently, global fishes drink polluted warer or eat polluted food. They will have poison. SO, human will have high chancc to cat poison polluted fishes, due to fishes are poison or are polluted. So, human is doing foolish activities, we only hope to find oil exploration places to pollute ocean or we only spend money to buy ticket to catch ships to travel anywhere in global ocean. All of these human foolish behaviors will bring pollution to global ocean. On consequently, we will need to compensate to eat polluted or dirty or poision fishes, ourselves bodies health will be bad. In long time, we need have high chance to pay medical expenditure when we are old. So, pollution case may be one good example to explain how and why human foolish behavior may influence ourselves future need to compensate serious medical loss.

All of these human foolish behavior will bring pollution to global ocean. On consequently, we will need to compensate to eat polluted or dirty or poison fished , ourselves bodies health will be bad. In long time, we will have high chance to pay medical expenditure, when we are old. So, pollution case may be one good example to explain how and why human ourselves intellectual or foolish behaviors may influence future long time economic loss or economic growth or recession in micro and micro economic view.

On another water pollution aspect hand, if we often keep rubbish to sea, oil exploration processing pollutes ocean and ships‘ gas pollute ocean, then fishes will eat polluted food and drink dirty water, due to fishes will eat polluted food and drink dirty sea water because the global ocean is polluted seriously.

In fact, because human only consider how to buy boats to carry on any leisure water activities, or catches cruises to travel on the sea. Also, oil manufacturers only consider any where to find oil exploratin places to manufacture oil products from ocean, when their pol exploration processes can plooute ocean. Consequently, global fishes drink polluted water or eat direty food. They will have poison. So, human will have high chance to eat poison fishes.

Otherwise, such as pollutin case, it can infuence inflation or deflation. Consequently, the reason indicates supply and demand theory. If air pollution is serious, then we will consider health issue, global cars demand number may be influenced to reduce, when global cars number demand will reduce, global car prices and supply number will need to change to fall down in order to attract or persuade global car consumers choose to make car purchase decision.

Hence, global car manufacture number and car price will be influenced to reduce, due to global air pollution issue. Consequently, deflation will occur because when the country citizen usually does not spend much extra saving money to buy car expensive goods. Money value will be low. Otherwise, if global cair pollution is not serious, human considers to buy cars to enjoy driving leisure lives. So, global car demand is influenced to increase , also global car price will also influenced to increase.

Consequently, gobal human will choose to buy cars to drive. Due to we accept to spend extra saving to buy expensive car goods. Car sale price and supply may be influenced to rise up. Money value is influenced to reduce. Inflation may be influenced, due to global car consumers number increases, we would not have extra money to spend easily. Car expensive goods expenditure influences our spending habit to avoid to make car purchase decision more easily. So, human intellectual or foolish activities may bring inflation or deflation consequency in possible indirectly in macro economic view.

On conclusion, above pollution case explain that how and why human intellectual or foolish economic behaviors may bring inflation or deflation consequency as wll as economic growth or recession consequency as well as any goods demand and supply increasing or decreasing consequency. It implies that human behavior may have indirect relationship to influence any goods demand and supply number to either increase or decrease result as well as any goods price will be influenced to increase or decrease in micro and macro economic view.

The relationship between social change and human behavior

Why does economic changes may influence human individual behavioral change? I shall attempt to indicate shopping behavior and staying at home behavior to explain their case and effect relationsip as below:

Human behavior can be influenced by economic change or economic change can be influenced by human behavior? Why does recession may influence consumers reduce shopping desire? In social recession suitation, it is possible that many people lose jobs suddenly, due to businessmen lose many customers. They need to make decision to reduce employees number in order to continue to keep businesses. Consequently, many firms (organizations) their employees may lose jobs. When they have much time, due to lose jobs, they will feel to avoid to spend too much time and money to go to shopping often. Many losing jobs people, they will often stay at homes. So, they will reduce time to go to shopping, then non essential products won't their preferable choice purchase products. Hence, recession will change many losing jobs people their shopping or consumption desires to avoid to buy non essential products often . Usually when economic boom, many people have jobs to do because consumers number must increase when many people have jobs to do. Then, many people can accept to spend money to buy non essential products often. Many people feel spend time to go to shopping can satisfy their purchase of any kinds of new products useful psychology or desire. So, recession is one good example to explain it can influence many people do not like often to leave homes to go to shopping easily. Many people like to stay at homes, becaue they feel worry about spending too much shopping time when they leave homes. Their staying home time is one good negative shopping behavior example. So,

economic change may influence human individual behavior changes , they have direct cause and efect relationship in behavioral economic view.
May human behavior influence economic change? Is it possible that human behavior may bring the country social economic change in macro economic or micro behavioral economic view ? I shall indicate publishing industry example. Do you feel that if there are many students feel learning is very important when they read many books or many of students feel interesting to read or they have reading new books in habit, then it is possible that the country will have many students like to spend time to go to any book shops to choose the books, they feel that they can help they learn new knowledge. Then the country will increase students number, they often spend time to visit any one book shop every week. Their visiting book shops behavior which may become their habits. So, the country will increase students number, they often spend time to visit book shops. Also, it implies that visiting book shops behaviors may be their behavioral habits.
So, when the country has many students often spend time to visit book shops , their visiting book shops behaviors may help any one book shop to raise books sale chance. So, the country's student individual often visiting book shop behaviors, their habitual visiting book shops behaviors must may assist help any one book shop to increase books sale number absolutely.
Consequently, any one book shop , its books sale bumber must be influenced to increase to increase because the country will have many students like or feel need visit book shops habit in order to choose any suitable books to buy to read at home in order to raise themselves learning effort. When the country has many bok shops often have many students visit their book shops, then their books sale number may be influenced to increase. It explain why student individual visiting book shop behavior may help any one book shop sale number increases also.

How human productive behavior may influence economic development

May any country which citizen behavior assist themselves country development? It is one cause and effect economic question. I mean that if the country itself citicen can not concentrate mind or energy to choose to do one kind of industry in order to let themselves country can bring the most benefit, then whether the counry itself economy can bring the most serious economic benefit. I shall attempt to indicate these countries themselves indistry choice to explain whether these countries themselves citizen productive behavior may help themselves countries to achieve the largest economic benefits. I shall indicate as below:

New Zealand farmer individual wine productive behavior

For New Zealand country example, this country concerns itself effort is foucs on farming agricultural aspect. So, this country has many farmers concentrate on farming agricultural aspect. May New Zealanders choose to spend time to produce different kinds of wines, e.g. wine or red grape wine is for the people are eating meat, or they are eating dinner.

When these New Zealanders their behaviors choose to do farming or agriculture to grow and produce different kinds of taste of white or red grape wine drinking products job. Themselves grape agriculture behavior will influence these New Zealanders themselves, they can learn how to improve different kinds of grape wine drinking products in order to achieve every kinds of white or read grape wines taste improving aim during their white or red grape producing process.

Why can New Zealander every individual white or read grape wine producers improve their white or read grape wine taste more easily? In behavioral economic view, it can explain that why any one New Zealander white or read grape wine producer can be encouraged or excited or persuaded to concentrate nervous and energy and effort to learn how to improve their white or red grape wine products easily.

In fact, New Zealand is one agricultural food export country. It has good natural environment resource , e.g. land, seed to provide any one farmer to produce themselves any kinds of agricultrual food products, e.g. fruit, or wine food products. Because New Zealanders know themselves country has enough natural resource . So, in common, many New Zealanders choose to attempt to do farming agricultural jobs in order to export themselves any kinds of fruit or meat or wine products to overseas or sell to domestic in order to earn profit.

So, when these New Zealand farmers number has been increasing every year. This country farmers will feel themsleves competition between this New Zealand farmers themselves are serious due to they may feel New Zealanders choose to do agriculture businesses in order to export themselves different kinds of farming food to overseas or sell to local to earn profit.

Hence, when many New Zealand farmers feel that farmers number has been increasing every year. They will feel themselves competition is serious. They must need to spend much time and nervous and effort to research what method is the best how to produce the best taste of white or red grape wine products in order to let local or overseas wine buyers to choose to buy his/her producing white or read grpae products to drink.

Hence, in competition psychological view, may influence many New Zealand white or reaad wine producers had been beginning to change their learning behavior on researching what method is the best in order to produce the best quality of taste red or white wine products to sell in order to attract overseas or local white or read grape wine drinkers to choose to buy his/her wine products. Their behavior will focus on learning how to raising or improving white or read grape wine taste method more than only focus on producing a large number white or red grape wine products. They believe wine quality is more important to compare wine producing number. So, New Zealand wine producers themselves wine producers behaviors have been changing on concentrating on researching wine quality method aspect more then wine producing number aspect in behavioral economic view.

America high technological productive behavior

For America example, US is one high technological country, it owns many high technological knowledge talent inventors, e.g. computer science inventors. Hence, US must attract many diferent countries owning high technological computer inventors choose to go to US to develop their computer science profession career. Also, it seems that when many computer science inventors or professions choose to go to US to develop themselves computer science new career. In behavioral economic view, due to their leaving themselves countries choice, which may bring influence themselve country job behaviors need to be changed. They must need to adapt US new live. Because they will forgive their past computer science job. These computer science professionals need to spend time to adapt US new lives. They " past computer science job behaviors" will need to be changed to their new US any computer employer's new computer science job model.

Because their traditional computer science jobs needed to be forgot in their themselves countries. They will feel their old computer science job knowledge and behavior needed to change in order to let their US any one new of computer company employer feels satisfactory to accept their new working behavior in any one US computer organization.

So, on the other hand, many US computer company employer will feel that they must need time to accept any one new overseas computer science professions their working behaviors, their working attitude daily, because these foreign comouter science professional, their past computer working behaviors and working attitude must be different to US domestic computer science professions.

In behavioral economic view, these overseas computer science professions, their working behaviors and attitude must be needed to change in order to adapt any one US new computer company itself domestic or local computer science professional stafs themselves daily working behaviors and attitude because these overseas and local computer science professionals must need to team work together.

In behavioral economic view, it is only one way that foreign computer science professionals must need to change themselves past country traditiona daily working behaviors and attitude in order to cooperate with these US local computer science professionals in teams more easily.

Consequently, if these foreign compute science professionals can change their past working behaviors and attitude to let any one US local computer science professional feels to cooperate with them easily in short time. Then, the US computer company itself whole computer professional teams themselves efficiencies will be influenced to raised or improved by the changing past working attitude and working behaviors of these foreign computer science professionals. So, in behavioral economic view, only if US any one computer company hopes itself computer teams themselves efficiency can be raised or improved when it decides to employ foreign computer science professionals and US domestic computer science professionals. They need to work in teams together. They must need to let these foreign computer science professionals to know how to change their working behaviors and attitude to let their domestic computer science professionals feel easy to work together. Then, the US computer company itself whole team efficiency must be rasied or improved easily in short time.

- China share market investing behavior

For China share market example, economic development depends on financial market. Because if many Chinese have interest to invest to carry on shares buying and selling activities in orde to learn how to earn shares interest and share profit when the China shareholder can make decision to sell himself/herself shares in the the high price, then he/she can earn money when he/she can sell the China company's shares in the high sale share price position.

If China has many Chinese like to spend time to carry on investing shares activities. Themselves shares buying and selling behaviors will influence China has many companies can increase fund from many Chinese shareholders in order to have enough money to expand or develop themselves businesses in China in long term.

Consequently, when China can have many Chinese like to attempt to carry on buying and selling shares investing behaviors in China share market. Themselves buying and selling shares behaviors can help many Chinese companies have effort to increase enough money or capital in order to continue to do their businesses in long term absolutely. So, it explains why when many Chinese become shareholders , they can assist China will have many companies continue to develop their businesses if many Chinese like to carry on shares buying and selling investing behaviors in long time in China financial investment market nowadays in behavioral economic view.

Why has any individual country have many people invest share behavior which can influence the country's macro consumption desire?

I shall apply shares market buying and selling investment behavior to explaiin why shares investment behavior which may impact the country's overal consumption desire as below:

In behavioral economic view, I assume that when the coutry has many people have interest to attempt to carry on shares buying and selling investment behavior, then their frequent shares buying and selling behaviors which may bring negactive consumption desire or shopping desire of these shares investors their consumer behavior.

The reason is simple, when the country has many share buyers number suddenly been increasing rapidly. Consequently, these large group share investors must need to spend much time to research any kinds of company shares variations, whether when their share prices will rise up of fall down in order to achieve buying the company's shares in the lowest price and selling the company's shares in the highest price level in order to earn profit.

Basic on this reason, they must need to spend much extra time to research share prices changing behavior every day, e.g. one working person will wait to leave his/her job, after he/she can spend time to gather data to research the day's share price changing behavior after dinner. So, the working person's right time may be his/her share price market research behavior. Before he/she may spend his/her night time to go to shopping after dinner, but nowadays, he/she will fogive to do his/her shopping behavior before dinner or after dinner at hight sometime. He/she will make decision to spend much night time to turn on computer to click on share market website to research his/her share purchase choice to investigate whether

his/her share price whether it rises up or falls down at the moment in order to make his/her share buying or selling decision at ever night time.
I mean the when the country has many people are share investors, their shares investment behavioral spenging time which will influence many shops lose customers at might often because the country will have many people feel need to spend night time to turn on computer or watch television to investigate share price variation. So, the country will have many people / share investors choose to stay at home in order to carry on share price variation investigation behavior, they need to listen share market update news from radios or watch the share market update news from computer or TV at home every night. Consequenly, they must reduce times to leave themselves homes at night. So, their shopping behavior also will be reduced. Because these share investors feel need to spend time to investigate share price variation news at homes which can bring economic benefits (high opportunity benefits) when they choose to forgive to leave homes to go to shopping times (opportunity cost) every night.
On conclusion, it seems that when the country has many people are share investors, then their share price investigating behavior may bring negative shopping emotion at night. Consequently, the country's any one shop may lose many customers from this share investor consumer group in behavioral economic view. Hence, when the country's share investors number had been increasing rapidly, it will influence any shops lose many customers from this share investing customer group at night frequenly in short time, even long time in behavioral economic view, because their shopping desires or shopping emotion will be brought negative feeling when they make decisions to spend much time to listen radios or watch TV or computers share price update nes at night. Hence, share market will bring negative impact to influence consumer shopping desire or negative shopping emotion in bchavioral economic view.

Can technology influence human shopping behavioral change?
Nowadays, technological development has reached mature stage, whether technological mature stage may bring positive or negative shopping emotion influence to global consumers. I shall aplly internet inventin or ecommerce shopping channel tool to explain whether internet technology can bring postive or negative influence to global consumer behavior in behavioral economic view.
Internet is a good technological tool, it brings e-commerce business chance.

In fact, commonly, global has have many businessmen choose to use internet channel to carry on their products transactions between global online-buyers and their electronic websites. So, global many shoppers had begun to feel online shopping is more convenient to compare visiting shops shopping. Their shopping behaviors have been changed from internet technological tool. Global has many shoppers choose to buy any products from any overseas or local businessmen their web stores. They only need to spend time to find any businessmen their webstores to choose the most suitable products to pay visa to buy from their webstores. at homes. So, in general, global had have may shoppers had changed their shopping behaviors from visiting shops to visiting webstores at homes often.

So, it seems that internet technological tool had influenced global many shops disappear, but internet webstores will be replaced their actual shops on streets. Some of businessmen either they choose webstores to replace shops or choose websotes and shops both or still keep shops only. Hence, internet tool influences global businessmen have three kinds of products sale channels to let globa local and overseas consumers to choose how to buy their products.

However, in fact, many of global shoppers, youngers and olders had begun to accept to buy any products from webstores. They feel to spend time to leave homes to visit shops , their shopping behaviors will be wasted time to not essential part to their daily lives. Hence, since internet technological invention, it had changed many consumers their traditional visiting shops shopping habit to change to buying products from webstores channel.

However, on the one hand, internet creates webstores ecommerce shopping channel to let global many consumers do not need to leave homes to go to shopping. It brings negative visiting shops shopping emotion to global general consumers nowadays. But on the other hand, it also brings positive visiting internet webstores shopping emotion to global general consumer nowadays. So, it seems that global many consumers feel that they often do not need to spend much time to go out shopping. Many global consumers feel convenient and enjoy to choose any products to buy from different internet webstores, when the online buyer chooses the most suitable product, he she only needs to pay visa card to buy the product from the online seller's webstore conveniently at home.

Hence, online shopping can bring economic benefit to online buyers, e.g. avoiding walking time or spending transport fare to visit the shop to go to shopping, shortening or reducing shopping time to do another important

matter.
On conclusion, global many consumers began feel online shopping can bring more economic benefits on shortening shopping time, avoiding transport fare spending aspect. So, online shopping will be popular shopping behavior for future long time. It may encourage global many shoppers can make rapid shopping decision in short time in order to carry on any products buying transaction to global any one online shopper in short time easily in behavioral economic view. So, global many businessmen had begun to build themselves one attraction webstore in order to persuade different countries consumers to choose to click themselves webstores from internet channel to buy any kinds of products in short time easily.
So, internet technology had changed consumers traditional shopping behaviors to build positive online shopping emotion as well as raise online sellers' any products sale chance easily in behavioral economic view.

Why and how human behavior may influence the country's economic growth or recession?
When one country has many people choose to do the same matter for one period, whether their behavior may influence the country's pvera; economic growth or recession . I shall attempt to indicate cases toexplain their relationship as below:
For flowing rubblish behavioral case example, do you feel that when the country has many people often flow rubblish on the streets, instead of their flowing rubblish behavior may bring streets dirty? But, their flowing rubblish behavior may explain that this country has people may have enough money to buy food to ear, or enough cloths to wear, enough bottles of water to drink, even they may have enough money to buy new television, radio, refrigeraters , washing machines, desktops or laptops electronic home products from old to new to use in order to satisfy their living needs. So, when they flow old electronic home products, their flowing old home electronic products behaviors may seem that they have enough money to buy other new home electronic products to replace old home electronic products to use at homes.
However, it seems thaat this country ought have many people have jobs to do. So, many of them, they can easy to make purchase decison to flow any old home electronic products and buy any new home electronic products to use . Because this country has many people have jobs to do. So, they can often not use old home electonic products to become rubblishs to flow on streets after they had bought any kinds of new home electronic homes.

In fact, it also implies that this country's economy grows rapidly. So, many businesses can glow up rapdly. When they expanded their businesses, they must need to increase employees number in order to let they help themselves to raise productivity or serve their clients absolutely. So, when the country has many businesses can grow up, it seems that its economy must be better or it is improved to compare past. Due to many different kinds of home electronic products had been often bought to use by this country people in this period. So, this country's any streets can be observed that expensive electronic home products were flowed on streets anywhere. then, this country will have many electronic home products sellers can sell their home electronic products very easily. When this country has many people can find any kinds of jobs to do easily. So, due to unemploymen rate had been decreasing.

In behavioral economic view, as this many electronic home products rubblish country case, we can observe this country may have many people have jobs to do. So, consumption number has been increased long time. So, cheap food, or expensive home electronic products may be rubblish on any streets. This country's people , their flowing rubblish behaviors may be explained that many of people have enough jobs to do, so they have ability to buy any good taste food to eat or buy any kinds of expensive electronic home products to use. So, this country's economy may be improved for this long period. So, in behavioral economic view, when this country can have many electronic home products rubblishs are flowed on anywherer in streets frequently. It seems that this country will have many people have jobs to do, so it causes they often change old home electronic products or replaced them easily, when they have enough income to spend to buy any kinds of new home electronic products to use at homes easily. Moreover, their flowing old electronic home products behaviors also indicate that this country has many people their salaries may be increased in possible from their emplyers. When this country can have many different kinds of home electornic products are sold. It means that this country's electronic home products needs or demand had been increasing, due to many people have jobs to do and income increases to excite their living of needs also improve. Consequently, this country may seem have better economic improvement. We can observe from this country's electronic home products rubblish increasing income in theis period.

On conclusion, this country ought experience economic growth at this period. So, " flowing expensive electronic home rubblish increasing number

" may seem that this country's economic growth is rapidly in this period, due to many people have jobs to do as well as salaries increase in this period.

Technology how impacts human behavior changing?
Technology how influences human behavior to bring changing? For example, online share purchase and sale transaction from smart phone brings share investor can do share buying or selling transation in any where and any time conveniently, non manual driving auto vehicle, bring car owner feels comfortable and spends free time to do other matter, e.g. reading, listening mucis in himself or herself car freely. electrical energy vehicle can help car owner to reduce air polluton and it can brings the drivers do not feel drive long time in any journeys in order to avoid air pollution for environmental protection responsible car drivers in our societies. Thus, they will drive long time in any journeys when they can drive electronic energy cars to replace oil energy cars.
However, online technology can also bring consumers can choose to stay at homes to buy any things from seller individual online webstore conveniently. Such as online technology can bring shoppers do not need to spend much time to visit shops to buy any things. They can choose any kinds of products from any online sellers individual online webstores conveniently at homes. Online technology excite busy consumers can make purchase decision easily as well as it can help online sellers sell any kinds of products from internet easily.
In behavioral economic view, technology can change human behavior to be improved, it can let human feels comfortable, more free time ro use, rapid making any decisions, such as apply smart phones to make share purchase or sale transaction decision, online shopping decision, even travelling any where decision in short time, when the traveller finds the most cheap hotel accommodation room price and air ticket price frm any travel agent online tourism webstore, then the potential travel customer can follow the online hotel accommodation price and air ticket price data to make decision when to buy the air ticket from the airline travel agent or make decision when to prebook which hotel accommodation room to go to the country to travel from online travel agent tourism webstores. So, technology can encourage global any country travelers to make anywhere to trvel rapidly. If the traveler can find the country's general hotel rooms and airline tickets prices had been decreasing more sightly. The traveler may make travel decision to choose the country to travel in short time, then he/she can

prebook the country;s any hotel room and airline ticket to pay by visa fraom the country's any hotel and airline travel agent webstores., before one week, even one month or more easily. Hence, online technology can also encourage traveler individual frequent travel times to be increased, due to global travelers can find any hotel rooms and airline tickets prices from internet conveniently at homes. They do not need to spend time to visit any airline travel agent to enquire travel choice country's hotel rooms prices and airline ticket prices. They can compare global travel of countries choices ' all hotels rooms and airline agents air tickets prices to make prebook airline seat and hotel room decision before one week, one month even six months early.

On conclusion, online technology can encourage global travelers can make travelling any where and when traveling time desicions easily. It can excite tourism industry develops in long time. Also, such as electricity cars invention can encourage environment protection car owners do car purchase decision easily, because they can choose to drive electronic energy cars to replace oil energy cars in order to avoid air pollution occurs easily. So, electronic cars can increase electronic car purchasrs number, due to many of environmental protection attitude of car owners can choose to drive electricity cars to bring air cleans, even non -manual driving cars can encourage lazy driving and free time driving car owners to choose to buy non-manual (artificial intelligent) cars to drive , because they can spend much free time to read, listen music or do any matters in themselves cars, they do not need to drive cars, robotic (AI) auto driving machine is such one non-manual driver to help them to drive themselves cars confidently. So, non-manual driving cars can attract lazy and enjoying free time driving car owners to choose to buy to replace traditional manual cars to drive easily. Moreover, online share transaction can help any share investors to make share buying and selling decision in short time easily. When they can apply smart phones technological tool to carry on share buying and selling activities easily. They can observe any share rising or falling price suitation from smart phones in any where any any time easily. So, smart phone technology can help global any shareholders to make share purchase and sale transaction easily. So, technology can encourage human makes decision in short time rapidly.

How and why employees behaviors may influence economy development?

In behavioral economy view,I believe the country's any organizational employees behavior may bring indirect relationship to influence the country's long term economic development. I shall indicate past manufacture industry social development period to explain their relationship. For many countries' past business activities had belonged to manufacturing industry, such as US, UK past before 1980 year, it focused on steel manufacturing and steel manufacturing related machine products. So, US, Uk developed countries manufacturing industries may be past main country's economic income sources. I assume US , UK past had one million number different kinds of industries. They ought had about seven houndred thousand number organizational businesses were belonged to manufactured industry. They may include:

Steel manufacturing and steel related machine manufacturing, e.g. vehicle manufacturing, home appliances, e.g. washing machine, television, radio, refrigerate cooler, heater, air condition etc. different kinds of different kinds of steel -related manufacturing machine, they were manufactured from US, UK steel machine manufacturers. So, US, Uk the other three hundred thousand number industry may be general service industry, e.g. hotel service, restaurent, cinema, public transport service, tourism lesiure , wine bar, supermarket etc. different kinds of non-manufacturing industries business organizations were operated in UK, US past before 1980 year.

So, in UK, US developed countries industry development history, they ought have high percentage of businesses belonged to steel related manufacturing machine and steel products. Also, in the past before 1980 year, US, Uk business employers , they employed many workers are manufacturing workers. They needed to spend long time to work in factories. They were skillful workers, and they are trained to manufacturing cars, washing machine, television, heater, etc. even steel itself different kinds of steel related products to prepare to deliver to their shops to sell to US, Uk local or overseas clients.

So, I believe that past UK, US ought employ many employees, they belonged to skillful manufacturing workers, manufacture increasing steel machine or steel related machine number of products rapidly daily. So, if UK, US had had many of these manufacturing factories owned high skillful workers, then their manufacturing steel-related machine or steel both kinds of products number must be influenced to raise rapidly. Consequently, their steel machine manufacturing products would been exported to overseas or would been sold to local both markets , they may be influenced to raise sale number. They (these manufacturing workers) needed to be trained to know how to manufactur these different kinds of machine products in the efficient teams and they ought to be trained to raise their efficiencies in order to shorten time to manufacturing many kinds of steel related manufacturing machine or steel itself products rapidly. So , if their efficiencies and manufacturing performance was improved, these US, UK any one manufacturing worker and their teams ought achieve raising productivities significantly.

Hence, when past UK, US manufacturing industry development period, if these two countries‘ any manufacturing factories could have many manufacturing workers could be trained to be skillful and proficient manufacturing workers. Then, in past every day to these factories workers, they ought help their steel or steel related manufacturing employers to raise any kinds of machine or steel products number in every team. So, when past in the manufacturing industry development, US, UK could have many factories' manufacturing workers themselves steel or steel related machine products manufacturing skill could be trained to to improve to any kinds of these machine or steel manufacuring products quality as well as their products number could be influenced to raise by themselves skillful improvement significantly every day.

Then, what would be influenced to occur to past UK, US manufacturing industry period? In behavioral economic view, when these two manufacturing industry developed countries, such as UK, US , if they had many factories workers can be trained to improve their skill in order to achieve any kinds of steel or steel-related machine products quality could be improved as well as products manufacturing number could be also increased absolutely.

In consequence, past UK and US both countries ought increase themselves any kinds of steel and steel related machine products number to be supplied to themselves local shops to let local clients to choose any one kind of machine manufacturing products to buy easily as well as they could also export to supply overseas any countries to buy their different kinds of steel or steel related machine products to let overseas steel or steel related manufacturing machine product buyers, they can have many of these different kinds of these steel or steel-related different kinds of manufacturing machine from UK and UK these both countries easily to compare other countries.

On conclusion, I believe that past US, and UK macro manufacturing industry income GDP would increase significantly. So, they would have good economic growth performance because when many of these manufacturing workers themselves manufacturing effort could be improved. So, it explained when employees manufacturing abilities can influence economic growth indirectly.

Robots invention whether they can help organizations to raise efficiencies or inefficiencies?

In behavioral economic view, in any organizations, when the organization hopes its worker teams can raise efficiencies , the organization may choose to increase more workers number and/or it can provide training to improve these workets themselves skills in order to raise their efficiencies. For one warehouse example, when the warehouse increases many goods , they are needed to delivered these goods from the shelves to the delivering destination locations. If this warehouse supervisors feel these workers themselves goods delivery speeds are slow, which is possible due to this warehouse's workers number is not enough. So, this warehouse supervisor ought increase workers number in order to increase their goods delivery speed in order to deliver goods from the shelves to every indicated goods delivery destination in order to let any one lorry driver can transport the right kinds of goods and ensure the accurate goods number to transport to any one client home rapidly.

However, if this warehouse supervisor planed to buy several warehouse goods delivery robots to assist these warehouse workers to find the right kinds of goods from shelves and then deliver to the right destination location in the warehouse. So, these warehouse orkers can concentrate on counting the accurate goods number and ensuring the right kinds of goods in order to prepare to let lorry drivers to transport these goods to these goods of buyers themselvers homes rapidly. Consequently, in the first step, robots can concentrate on finding th right goods from shelves and delivers them to the right goods transportation of location destination. Then, in the second step, these warehouse workers can concentrate on counting the accurate goods number and ensuring the right kinds of goods in order to prepare to put them to the lorry. Consequently, when warehouse robots and warehouse workers can cooperate to work together, the most important, robots, can deal on finding the right kinds of goods and deal on delivering the accurate number of goods of job duty as well as these warehouse workers can only concentrte on counting the right kinds of goods number in order to avoid it has none any mistake of wrong kinds of goods and inaccurate goods of delivery number to be transported to the lorry and to deliver to any one buyer's home.

So, it seems that warehouse robots ought help any one warehouse worker to raise himself efficiency and avoid goods delivery of mistake occurrence easily as well as their help to warehouse workers that can let any one goods buyer feels their goods can be delivered to their homes rapidly. Moreover, warehouse robots can also help these warehouse workers to raise efficiencies because warehouse robots can help them to shorten goods delivery time between any one shelf and any one goods delivery destination of location in the warehuse because robots may help them to find the right kinds of goods from the right shelf in the short time. So, any one worker does not need to spend long time to seek anywhere is the right shelf location for the kind of goods when the kind of goods are needed to deliver to the buyer's home from lorry. Warehouse robots can help them to do this aspect of " finding the goods from the right shelf in short time job duty". So, any one warehouse worker only needed tospend less time to do the counting of any right kind of goods number and ensuring the right kind of goods job duty. Consequently, this warehouse 's any one worker, his any one kind of goods delivery time may be reduced, because robots' assistance and they may have more confidence to avoid mistake to deliver the wrong number of goods and/or the wrong kind of goods to any one goods buyer's home.

On conclusion, it seems that warehouse robots ought may help any one warehouse worker to raise efficiency for any one team in the warehouse as well as the warehouse any one supervisor does not need to spend much time to observe any one worker individual performance for " goods delivery job duty aspect" because their goods delivery job duty that had been replaced to do by these several warehouse robots. Robots can achieve the more accurate of right kinds of goods and the right number of goods delviery job performance to compare any one of human warehouse worker themselves right kinds of goods of delivery and right number of goods of delivery job performance. So, when robots can participate to cooperate with this warehouse's any one worker to do their goods of delivery job duty in this warehouse every day. Then, robots can raies any one of supervisor individual confidence in order to let they do not need to spend time to observe any one of worker individual whose goods of delivery job performane. They can concentrate on supervising any one worker whose goods transport to lorry in the final step in order to avoid to deliver wrong goods number and / or wrong kind of goods to any one goods buyer's home every day. Consequently, this warehouse's overall teams of their delviery of goods performance many be improved by robotss' participatin to goods of delivery task as well as this warehouse's oveall teams themselves efficiencies may be influenced to raise by robots' goods of delivery task participation.

Why social behavior may influence organizational strategy needs to be changed ?

Why any organizations need to know whether nowadays social behaivor how has been changing in order to implement the kind of the most right strategy to achieve the profit aim pursue in possible. I shall indicate nowadays ecommerce or online, customer shopping behavior to explain above question concerns they ought have close relationship between social behavior and organizational strategic choice or organizational behavioral changing need.

On nowadays ecommerce business, or online shopping model, this kind of shopping model in global many young and old age consumers like to apply internet tool to choose any country sellers website stores in order to stay at home to buy any kinds of products from themselves webstores in global societies.

In fact, online shopping model had been popular for long time above to twenty years. Most of global sellers will make decision to design themselves webstores in order to attract global many online buyers to choose to buy their products from themselves webstores. So, it seems that social consumers purchase behaviors had been changed to online shopping from internet invention.

Hence, social consumers purchase behavioral changes may influence any organizations' strategies need to be changed from visiting shops purchase strategy model to online purchase strategy model, if the seller still concentrate on concentrate on considerate how to design itelf , but neglects to considerate how to design itself webstore, e.g. how to design attract product photos to put on itself webstore, how to arrange sale price information location to be putted on webstore and visa card payment location on itself webstore in order to let any one online buyer can feel very easier to buy itself any kinds of products from itself webstore. Then, its potential online buyers will be influenced to increase number when they can find this online seller itself any kinds of products photes and every kinds of product sale price information and visa card payment channel locations easily from itself webstore.

So, it implies that nowadays any one seller ought need to design one webstore to let any one online overseas and domestic consumers can have chance to click itself webstore to choose any one kind of product to buy conveniently when he/she does not hope to leave him/her home to go to shop, because nowadays social shopping behaviors had been influenced to change when internet invention, them it gives another online purchase method to replace visiting shops purchase method to global any one buyer in nowadays societies.

So, if nowadays any one seller still concentrate on how to design itself shop display in order to put any kinds of product on shelf in order to let any one visiting shop customer to find the kind of product to buy, but it neglects to change to choose to pursue another new technological shopping method, such as webstore purchase method in order to implement effective strategy to design the most right webstore as well as in order to attract global overseas and local consumers to find itself webstore easily from website and find its any one kind of product phots and sale price and visa card payment button in order to choose to buy itself any kinds of products in the short time. Consequently I believe that the seller will lose many customers from overseas and local when its other same or similar product sellers choose to design themselves webstores in order to let global any one product buyer can buy themselves any one kind of product when they can pay visa card to buy their products from them webstores conveniently when they stay at home habitly. Then, the seller will lose many global potential customers in long time.

On conclusion, in behavioral economic view, any consumer behavioral social changing, which will influence any in order to avoid customers number loses significantly . In future time, organizations need to make rapid decision in order to implement the most reasonable and the most useful strategy in order to avoid global potential customers number reduces or lose them in long time. So, social behavioral changing environment ought influence any global organizations need to decide how to change themselves strategies in order to avoid customers loses significantly in future time.

How and why human behavior may influence economic growth or recession?

May ourselves daily behaviors influence our global societial continue economic growth or recession? Do they have cause and effect close relationship between human behaviors and global economic growth or recession? I shall apply behavioral economic theory to analyze and explain whether ourselves daily behaviors and our global societial economic growth or recession which have close cause and effect relationship as below:

Every country itself economic development must depend on any business activities, otherwise, any kinds of business activities must need ourselves business activities or behaviors in order to achieve any business activities as well as achieve the country's overall economic development in macro view. However, any country's overall business activites or behaviors which must depend on any kinds of individual businessmen, themselves employees daily working behavior or activity or performance in order to help them to attract or increase many clients number to acieve " earning profit" aim. So, it seems that any individual business, itself overall every department individual working behavior is one main factor to influence the company's overall business performance.

For agricultural fruit and meat food farming industry example, such as New Zealand is a farming main target industry country. It had had many New Zealanders were daily themselves own farming businesses for many years. Their farming businesses include growing fruit, sheep, cow, pig pork, meat etc. food sale business. If the New Zealand farmer owned a large size farming land, then he will choose either growing fruit or feeding sheeps, pigs, cows to be meat to to transport to New Zealand supermarkets to help them to sell to their farmers meet to New Zealanders in order to earn profit. Thus, if the New Zealand farmer owned large size of farming lands, then he needs to employ many farming employees (farming workers) to help him to carry on farming business daily tasks, e.g. picking up friuts, feeding pigs, cows, sheeps to eat food daily. These daily farming jobs are very important to influence this New Zealand farmer's meats or fruits sale number whether they can be easy or diffcult to sell in New Zealand supermarkets , if these farming workers can own encough farming knowledge or skill to know how to pick up fruits method and make judgement to know whether it is right time to pick up the kind of fruits from the trees , as well as know how feed this pigs, sheeps, cows to eat food in order to let they are better health. Consequently, their farming behaviors which can let these animals can provide the best taste and enough meat from these animals to let New Zealander to buy to eat from New Zealand any one supermarket. Even these New Zealand farming workers can know whether the kinds of fruits, e.g. oranges, apples, gapes etc. fruits whether they ought be picked up from the trees at the right time. Consequently, they can make judgement to decide to pick up any kinds of the best taste fruits to let any one New Zealander to buy to eat from any one supermarket in New Zealand. Otherwise, if they do not make judegement to know whether the kind of fruit ought not be picked up because they still need longer time to continue grow up to increase fruit size and better taste from the trees in order to let any one fruit buyer can feel better taste when they eat this kind of fruit later. If they can buy this kind of fruit to eat later, then this New Zealand farmer's his fruit buyers can buy the best taste of this kind of fruit to eat from an yone supermarket in New Zealand. Consequently, many New Zealand supermarkets will choose to buy any kinds of fruits from this farmer fruit supplier when they feel this farmer's fruits can provide more better taste fruits to compare other farmers' fruits.

Thus, due to New Zealand is one farming main income source country. It's any kinds of fruits and meats need to be export to overseas to sell , instead of local sale. It's GDP percent is very high to whole country 's overall income source. So, any one New Zealand farmer individual and any one farming worker individual working behavior will influence its economy whether it is influenced to grow or recession possible. Moreover, it also seems that farming workers' farming knowledge and skill will influence themselves farming daily activities to achieve the aim of the number of increase or decrease to any kinds of fruits whether they are better taste or the number of increase of decrease to any kinds of meats whether they are better taste to supply to any one New Zealand fruit or meat buyers to eat from any one New Zealand supermarket. So, it implies that any one New Zealand farming worker individual farming behavior may influence any kinds of fruits or any kinds of meat taste because they are transported to any one supermarket to sell in New Zealand.

Consequently, if New Zealans had many farmers can teach god farming knowledge and skill to let their any one farming workers know how to decide judgement to decide when it is right time to pick up any kinds of fruits from trees , or how to grow them on soil in order to let they can grow rapidly. Then, many different kinds of fruits can be provided to let any one New Zealanders can eat the best taste of fruits when their fruits are supplied to any one New Zealand supermarkets. Even, if they knew how to feed foods to pigs, cows, sheeps to eat daily. Then they can be more health and they can provide the best taste of meats to let any one New Zealanders can buy their meats from any one New Zealand supermarkets. Moreover, their fruits and meats can be transported to overseas to let any one country fruits or meats buyers can choose any kinds of New Zealand meats and fruits to buy to eat from themselves countries supermarkets. Then, many overseas fruit and meat buyers will perfer to choose New Zealand any kinds of fruits or meats to buy to compare other countries fruits or meats to buy when they go to any one local supermarkets.

On conclusion, it seems that New Zealand farming workers themselves farming behavior may influence their farming employers any kinds of fruits or meats sale number and income because their farming task behaviors must influence whether their fruits or meats taste are the better taste or worse taste to compare their other local farmers (the farmer competitors) whose fruits or meats taste. If tthe farmer's any one farming worker can be trained to learn how to know to feed animals skill and when is the most right time to pick up any kinds of fruits from trees or how to grow them on the soil methods. Due to these farming worker individual farming behavior may influence his different finds of fruits and meats sale number to be increase or decrease, so these any one New Zealand farmer must need to depend on any one farming worker whose farming working methods, if their farming working behaviors can be the best to influence any kinds of fruits to grow rapid or any kinds of pigs, cows, sheeps animals grow up rapidly , then their sale number may be increase significantly and their taste can be improved to let any New Zealand or overseas meat or fruit buyer to buy to eat to feel from any one New Zealand or overseas supermarkets, then New Zealand's agriculture industry must be influenced to increase. In the world, any one fruit or meat buyer must choose to buy New Zealand's fruit and meat to eat in prefer to compare other countries' fruits and meats. So, New Zealand's GDP may be influenced to raise from any one New Zealand farming worker individual farming working behaviors.

Reasons why human behavior may influence economic recession or growth?

Can ourselves daily behaviors or activies influence ourselves countries' economic growth or recession? I shall attempt to explain the reasons why they have direct or indirect relationship between human behavior and economy growth or recession as below:

I shall indicate environment pollution case to attempt to explain above question. Our societies had been experiencing servious environment pollution challenge. However, environment pollution , such as air pollution is caused by air planes and vehicles emission by air planes and vehicles emission as well as water pollution is caused by plastic rubblish, or dirty water or oil or gas chemical material, these both kinds of pollution ought may bring economic recession and this both kinds of pollution are caused by human ourselves daily foolish activities.

I believe human behavior and economy and pollution which have cause and effect relationship. I shall analyze this environment pollution case to explain why they have case and effect relationship between human foolish behavior and environment pollution and economic recession as below:

When global societies had many people like to buy cars to drive to bring emission to fresh air on the roads as well as many manufacturing factories will bring emission to pollute fresh air in their manufacturing processes. Factories and cars will bring air pollution , due to factories need to pollute fresh air in order to manufacture many products and car owners need to drive their cars to go to offices or leisure places. Their cars will also bring emisson to pollute fresh air. On consequence, car owners themselves frequent driving behaviors and factory workers themselves frequent manufacturing behaviors may bring environment pollution. Technology or human behavior whether may influence economic growth or recession. Moreover, air planes also brings emission to pollute air when they are flying in sky. Also, when ships bring oil pollution or sea plastic rubblishs bring pollution to global oceans.

In fact, manufactuers and cars owners, such as factories workers manufacturing behaviours ans car owners driving behaviors and pilots driving air planes flying behaviors and ships transport behaviors, which may cause plastic rubblish, oil or gas emission to sky or sea or on the road to cause ocean and air pollution is serious. However, human ourselves need to buy cars to drive to satisfy ourselves driving leisure or enjoyment, travelers need to catch air planes to travel to enjoy leisure needs, factories workers need help factories to manufacture many products to sell to customers to satisfy their using needs. oil exploration needs to find lands to explore new oil lands.

All of these business and leisure activites may bring serious air and water pollution. However, due to serious air and water pollution will bring earth warming challenge , such as some countries temperature will be influences to rise up to 40 degree or higher br earth warming. However, earth warming is caused by air and ocean pollution. Pollution must be caused by human ourselves, driving cars leisure and factories manufacturing business activities. Hence, if human decided to continue to do these foolish behaviors, we only pursue to manufacture different kinds of industrial products or drive cars to enjoy leisure aims, but we also neglect ourselves behaviors may bring environment pollution. Then, earth warming or earth temperature will be influenced to rise up absolutely in long term. Moreover, if our future earth will be influenced to bring serious high temperature effect by human ourselves these foolish behaviors.

On consequencey, warth warming will bring serious economic losses in possible because when ourselves earth temperature had been influenced to rise up to 40 degree or high. Ourselves health will be caused poor, due to we will feel difficult breath, we must need often tried and hard to work, due to our nervous and health will be influenced to poor by pollution and earth warming effect. Also, we need to pay more money to see doctors when we had long life. Then, our societies will lose may strong labors to help manufacturers to work, e.g. factories will reduce workers number to help manufacturers to produce more different kinds of products, due to workers health is general poor. Due to lacking enough workers to manufacture products, our societies will begin to reduce enough supply number of products to sell to global consumers to satisfy their use needs.

On conclusion, in behaviroal economic view, our societies will lose many labors due to their bodies are not health by air and water pollution. Global economic and business activities will be influenced to worse by global workers reducing number reason. So, economic recession will begin to occur in possible when pollution reaches the serious level.

CHAPTER FIVE

Persuading traveller space travel leisure choice

The comparison benefit
and risk between space
travel and space exploration

When our money, time, technological resource, human resource is shortage, whether we ought concentrate on investing space travel entertainment and space exploration or choice of either one investment only. We need to evaluate whether future how much benefit we can earn more between either space travel and space exploration as well as whether what we will encounter more failure risk between space travel and space exploration. Hence, I feel that space scientists need to compare their benefit and risk both in order to concentrate on choosing only one implementation.

In prior , I shall indicate what the space exploration benefits and risks are. Latter I shall indicate what the space travel benefits and risks are. What does space exploration mean? Space exploration is the use of astronomy and space technology to explore outer space. physial exploration of space is conducted both by human spaceflights and by robotic spacecraft. There are different types of exploration? They may include:
•Arctic exploration •Cave exploration •Desert exploration •Mineral exploration •Ocean exploration •Space exploration •Urban exploration •Mountain exploration these different kinds of exploration. I feel space exploration will bring these possible benefits and risks as below:

On job creation aspect

The possible of space exploration may include as these: the popularly cited benefit of space exploration is "job creation", or the fact that a space agency and its network of contractors, universities and other entities help people stay employed. From time to time, NASA puts out figures concerning how many associated jobs a particular project generates, or the economic impact. Employment can also be full-time, part-time or occasional. So while "job creation" is cited as a benefit, more details about those jobs are needed to make an informed decision about how much good it does.

On education aspect

Teaching has a high priority for NASA, so much so that it has flown astronaut educators in space. (The first one, Christa McAuliffe, died aboard the space shuttle Challenger during launch in 1986. Her backup, Barbara Morgan, was selected as an educator/mission specialist in 1998 and flew aboard STS-118 in 2007.) And to this day, astronauts regularly do in-flight conferences with students from space, ostensibly to inspire them to pursue careers in the field. NASA's education office has three goals: making the workforce stronger, encouraging students to pursue STEM careers (science, technology, engineering and mathematics), and "engaging Americans in NASA's mission." Other space agencies also have education components to assist with requirements in their own countries. It's also fair to say the public affairs office for NASA and other agencies play roles in education, although they also talk about topics such as missions in progress.

On intangible benefits aspect

Added to this host of business-like benefits, of course, are the intangibles. What sort of value can you place on better understanding the universe? Think of finding methane on Mars, or discovering an exoplanet, or constructing the International Space Station to do long-term exploration studies. Each has a cost associated with it, but with each also comes a smidgeon of knowledge we can add to the encyclopedia of the human race. Space can also inspire art, which is something seen heavily in 2014 following the arrival of the European Space Agency Rosetta mission at Comet 67P/Churyumov–Gerasimenko. It inspired songs, short videos and many other works of art.

Instead of tangible and intangible aspects, space exploration may also include these advantages as below:

1. Space exploration allows us to prepare for potential hazards.

The universe is a vast place where hidden dangers could be lurking almost anywhere. Even if you consider only our solar system, there are asteroid and comet threats which could devastate our planet if an impact were to occur. Exploring space gives us an opportunity to locate these hazards in advance to prepare an encounter that could help to preserve our race. Then there are the interstellar items to consider. Oumuamua, or 11/2018 U1, was discovered by the Pan-STARRS1 telescope in 2017 by the University of Hawaii through funding from the Near-Earth Object Observations Program. It was originally thought to be an asteroid, then a comet since it was accelerating, and up to 10 times as long as it was wide. These items could create interstellar impacts as well.

2. It gives us more information about our solar system, galaxy, and universe.

When we take on the effort to start exploring space, then we can discover new truths about our planet and culture simultaneously. The information we obtain from these studies can then be applied to our STEM resources here at home. NASA technologies that were originally developed for space programs include infrared ear thermometers, LED lighting, ventricular-assist devices, anti-icing systems, and even temper foam. Because it requires us to innovate to reach to the stars, our efforts to solve critical problems create opportunities to make life better here on our planet at the same time.

3. Exploring space is one of the few human endeavors that crosses borders.

There are currently 72 countries who claim to have a space program, but there are only three which have an operating government space agency: China, Russia, and the United States. Despite the political conflicts that occur between these nations, their capability of producing human spaceflight provides the gold standard for future exploration efforts. Only 14 of the 72 nations who operate in this space even have a basic launch capacity and six (adding Europe, India, and Japan) have the capability to launch or recover multiple satellites. Because of the expenses and resources necessary to achieve space flight, the remaining nations work together with those who have the capability of a full launch to manage this aspect of human existence. This endeavor is one of the few ways that humans from all nations cooperate without conflict.

4. We can see humanity in a different way with space exploration.

Carl Sagan suggested that Voyager 1 take a picture of Earth while it was 4 billion miles away at more than 30 degrees above the ecliptic plane. In that image, our planet appears as a 0.12 pixel crescent. All of our conflicts, political battles, successes, failures, love, loss, and life occur on this one-tenth of a pixel. In the scope of a universal lens, we are but one small point of light amount countless others.

"Look again at that dot," wrote Sagan. "That's here. That's home. That's us. On it everyone you love, everyone you know, everyone you ever heard of, every human being who ever was, lived out their lives. The aggregate of our joy and suffering, thousands of confident religions, ideologies, and economic doctrines, every hunter and forager, every hero and coward, every creator and destroyer, every king and peasant... every saint and sinner in the history of our species lived there – on a mote of dust suspended in a sunbeam."

5. Space exploration provides us access to new raw materials or undiscovered natural resources.

When we began to launch satellites into space, it allowed us to find new raw material deposits on our planet that we could access to make life easier here. If we apply this technology as an extension to the rest of our solar system, then it gives us the same benefit to find minerals, precious metals, and even new materials that we can use. Although the expense of exploring space is admittedly high, this advantage gives us a way to offset those costs somewhat. There is even the potential that it could become profitable one day if we can provide these efforts with enough capital.

6. Investments into space exploration create real economic benefits at home.

The governments which provide the majority of our space exploration infrastructure employ over 20,000 people per agency who make direct positive economic impacts on their community. There are private companies who look at the potential benefits of this industry and contribute to this advantage as well, such as SpaceX and their thousands of staff. People from all walks of life contribute to space exploration every day, ranging from astronomers to actual rocket scientists. Even though many of these programs receive taxpayer funding, the wages, manufacturing, and indirect investments contribute over 70% more in overall value at the local level compared to each dollar spent in the United States. These opportunities allows us to explore many different fields of study in addition to what is waiting in the universe as well.

7. Anyone can become a space explorer to achieve their dream.

Space exploration doesn't need to involve starships, space stations, or intergalactic travel. If you own a telescope and can look up at the sky, then you can embrace this element of human existence. Our scientists have taken this advantage to the next level with the Hubble Space Telescope, which has made over 1 million observations in almost 30 years of service. We have made some incredible discoveries with this technology already.

•We have a better idea about the age of the universe (around 13.7 billion years).

•Images of the deep universe show that there are thousands of galaxies out there.

•It helped us to discover four of the five moons that orbit Pluto.

•We have a better understanding of planetary seasons in our universe.

•It works to peer into the atmospheres of alien planets so that we know what is waiting for us in our future exploration efforts.

8. Space exploration encourages us to share instead of being selfish.

Being human-first from a space exploration standpoint isn't about dominating other cultures that we might find waiting for us in the universe. It is a way for us to find common ground outside of our physical appearance, cultural differences, or religious preferences. For far too long, we have allowed ourselves to be consumed by our petty problems instead of looking at the big picture. If someone is hungry, then we should feed them. If they are cold, then we should clothe them. If they need a job, then we should help to train them. Space exploration unites us in ways that other global efforts do not because we see ourselves as humans first. This advantage won't solve our problems, but it can shift our attitude toward something that is healthier than our current state.

9. We know more about our planet thanks to our efforts to explore space.

Because space exploration gives us a different perspective, it allows us to look at our planet in a different way. The view from outside of our atmosphere allows us to see the big picture instead of trying to extrapolate information from micro-scale research. This advantage allowed us to discover the problem of ozone depletion in the upper atmosphere, begin the conversations on global warming, and examine the current and future impact of weather pattern changes that may happen because of a changing climate. Space exploration helps us to look inward as well as outward, helping us all to find the changes that are necessary to keep our planet healthy for our children, grandchildren, and beyond. But, space exploration also have these disadvantages, they may include as below:

1. Our current technology makes it dangerous to get into space in the first place.

Several agencies are developing "space tourism" packages that can take people in a comfortable aircraft to the very outer layers of our atmosphere, but that is not an exploration effort. We currently strap astronauts into a vehicle that gets attached to a very large rocket so that there is enough speed available to break the grasp of gravity.

Starting with Theodore Freeman, who was killed in the crash of a T-38 in October 1964, there have been over 20 individuals who lost their lives in the line of duty while advancing U.S. space program interests. There have been two individuals (Gus Grissom and Peter Siebold) who were able to survive a problem that resulted in the loss of a space vehicle.

2. There are cost considerations to look at with space exploration.

The cost of exploring space is one of the biggest criticisms of the efforts to launch a program that takes us beyond our planet. When the space shuttle program was active in the United States, the total cost of the launch was about $500 million. That figure does not include the expenses of postponement that often occurred because the conditions were not right to send a rocket into space.

Manned missions in our solar system could cost 10 times that amount, and that might get us to Mars or one of Jupiter's moons. Technology advancements in recent years could make this issue cheaper for the next generation, but we should ask ourselves if spending billions on space exploration is the right thing to do if we have people dying of hunger on our planet.

3. Astronauts receive exposure to natural dangers while in space.

If the launching process doesn't kill you during a manned space exploration effort, then the natural dangers that are present outside of our planet's atmosphere could become problematic in a variety of ways. The radiation that comes from the sun is a constant danger to astronauts when they are in space, and the weightless environment can change their physical conditioning. Experiments with identical twins, with one staying on our planet and the other spending a lengthy assignment in space, show that there are changes at the cellular and genetic level that occur with space travel as well.

4. Current space exploration efforts could be a one-way trip.

When we sent astronauts to the moon, our technology provided them with a chance to land on the surface and return to their spacecraft. It is possible that we could perform a similar action for asteroids, moons around other planets, and other celestial bodies that do not have an atmosphere. If we are going to start exploring Mars, then that journey could be a one-way trip for the astronauts. Even if this journey does not become a one-way trip, the amount of time necessary to reach a destination beyond the moon makes it virtually impossible to mount a rescue mission if something goes wrong. Our current vision of space exploration requires perfection to create a successful result.

5. There may not be a reason to start exploring at this time.

Human cultures have always had a fascination with exploring space because it satisfies our need to learn more about the universe. Taking long-distance pictures with the Hubble telescope is not the same as visiting the location in-person. What we must ask ourselves right now is if there is a valid reason to begin this effort, and the truth is that there are few pragmatic applications to consider. We could start mining asteroids for their raw materials and mineral content in the future. Planetary colonization could be necessary in future generations. Since we are still dealing with issues like crime and poverty here at home, addressing our immediate concerns might be better than looking at future needs which might never be necessary.

6. Unmanned probes are even a waste of resources.

One of the ways that we attempt to limit expenses with our space travel needs is to send unmanned probes into the dark vastness that lies beyond. There have been some successes with these efforts, most notably the Voyager 1 and Voyager 2 missions that allow us to peer outside of our solar system. This option allows us to almost eliminate the risk to human life entirely as well. There are also disadvantages to consider with this approach, starting with the fact that there is little adaptability to changing circumstances. The Mars Climate Orbiter is an excellent example of this problem. When it received incorrect coordinates for landing, it burned up while entering the atmosphere before sending any data at a cost of more than $120 million.

7. Our current information is well out-of-date.

On February 22, 2017, NASA announced that it had found seven planets the size of Earth in a single solar system. Three of the planets were in the so-called Goldilocks Zone, which means they are at a distance from their star that is not too hot and not too cold. It is called the Trappist-1 group, and this set of planets lies in the Aquarius system. That's about 235 trillion miles away, which is at least a measurable distance.

The problem is that this planetary system is 40 light-years away from us. That means the information that we can observe right now took forty years to get to our scientists. Think about all of the changes that have happened in your life in just the past 5 years, and then apply that concept to a planetary scale. When we start exploring space, we must take into account that this delay is present so that we don't fly into an unexpectedly dangerous situation.

8. It may lead us into future conflict with beings who have superior technology.

Space exploration makes us think in noble terms about what lies in wait for us in the universe. When we sent the Voyager spacecraft into our solar system and beyond, there were two records placed on the devices to communicate with whoever might find them to let that intelligent life know that we exist. Most theorists who seriously consider the pros and cons of meeting alien life say that there are only two possible outcomes that can occur with first contact. That alien species will either be so advanced that their technological presence as led to a peaceful society where an exchange of information may one day be possible, or it will be aggressive and want to access our planetary resources.

9. Space exploration creates a lot of trash or rubbish around our planet.

There are over half-a-million items of trash from over 50 years of space travel and satellite placement which orbit our planet right now. Unless these items fall into the atmosphere and burn up, they will stay in place forever. The ring of debris that we have created makes space exploration more dangerous because an impact with a ship's hull could have deadly results. We will need to clean up this mess in the future to provide better safety to our future explorers, and we have no idea what the expense might be.

Verdict (comparison) on the Advantages and Disadvantages of Space Exploration

Space exploration is beneficial even if we only look at it through the lens of hope. It is an idea that unites us as one race instead of over 190 different countries. We can proceed into the universe as one people, taking the first steps toward new experiences just like we did when we placed astronauts on the moon for the first time. Explorers always face danger, and space is no exception to that rule. The vacuum of the universe was not meant for humans, which means we must constantly adapt and protect ourselves when we are outside of our atmosphere. Then there is the risk of an encounter with alien life to consider too.

The advantages and disadvantages of space exploration must come from a common sense perspective. Other races could harm us, but there is also the possibility that we could be dangerous to other life as well. We should continue with these efforts, but with the understanding that this work is not a race. It is a cooperative effort that will eventually define our humanity.

Similarity, space exploration's benefit and risk may include as these: The benefits of space exploration is it helps man think outside the box as far as the dwindling resources are concerned. The risk is that it can lead to death. The only drawbacks are cost and safety. If you can afford the cost and are willing to take the risk, there are unlimited benefits. To further our knowledge on the ever expanding universes. However, there are so many problems that are associated with space exploration. Some of the problems include the high costs, the risk level is also very high and there are chances of getting negative results. But, space exploration also have these intangible benefits , such as the benefits are that it has more space and more fuel than the Apolo and it gives astronauts a chance to bring whole satilities. Space stations can help in the exploration of space because in space stations they do experiments on things they find in space.

How does space exploration impact us?

Beyond furthering the scientific understanding of how the universe formed, the mechanics involved in galatic, solar, and planetary formations, as well as mapping the universe for potential physical exploration at a later date, the space exploration programs impart a bevy of technologies which are applied to everyday use as well as research benefits that come from zero gravity research (such as medicines or materials development. The commercial impact seen from the space program can be possible brought to our next generation in the future. What are the reasons for space exploration? In conclusion, I feel that space exploration may bring these intangible benefits. they may include: Space exploration is an important part of our life today. The main reasons for exploring space are: The urge to know what is out there as well as by space exploration, we get to know if there is any harm from the heavens coming our way. Thus, space exploration will bring future intangible and tangible benefits more than present risk. Space scientists ought concentrate more nervous, time , human and technological resources to research how to achieve this space exploration mission more than space travel. Due to space travel present and future risk is more than future benefit as below reasons.

What are the benefits and risks of space travelling? I shall indicate as below:

What is space travel benefit ? Nowadays, human begins feel space travel is one kind of exciting entertainment activity, instead of earth travel. But, due to space travel cost is high, so this kind of travel activity is focus on rich people because they have more extra money to spend this kind of travel entertainment. It is its weakness. Space is fascinating. Humans have been sending objects into space for decades, trying to learn about Earth and what's beyond. But while space travel can be beneficial, there are also risks that come along with exploring the rest of the universe. There have been many more trips to space and the moon, as well as orbits around Earth. Our fascination with the universe beyond our own planet is as limitless as the universe itself. Technology and science have even allowed us to land on and explore Mars - a feat barely imaginable when space travel first began decades ago.

However, space travel also have these kinds of different risks when space travelers are flying rockets to space. The different risks may include as below:

(1) Health risk

The Health Risks of Space Travel

,research into the health risks of space travel may someday make long-duration spaceflights safer for astronauts. But despite such achievements, space travel still involves a myriad of health risks for people. From DNA damage caused by radiation exposure to the bone loss, muscle loss, and blood pressure changes that occur when living in microgravity, to name a few.

(2) Radiation risk

Also, space travel can bring radiation risks. The latest review examines eight NASA evidence reports, with half of the topics focused on the health risks of radiation exposure in space. "The radiation problem is the toughest one to solve and the most concerning," Valerie Neal, Ph.D., a historian at the National Air and Space Museum, told Health line. Neal spent 10 years working at NASA, but she was not involved in the current research. On Earth, Neal explained, we are shielded by the planet's magnetic field and the protective gases in the atmosphere.

However, there's no effective way to shield astronauts from some types of radiation present in space, especially on a long journey such as a trip to Mars.

In particular, there is no technology to protect against galactic cosmic rays, a type of ionizing radiation likely produced by supernovae, or exploding stars. That type of radiation can pass right through the hull of a spacecraft and the skin of people on board.

Astronauts also face radiation risks from solar particle events, which are difficult to predict.

In its current review, the National Academies' committee looked at NASA's evidence reports on radiation exposure and increased risk of cardiovascular disease, cancer, central nervous system disorders, and acute radiation syndrome. For the conditions covered in each report, the committee noted that NASA has well-documented evidence of the risks, although some studies rely heavily on animal models. One area of growing interest is the link between radiation and cardiovascular disease. The committee found that there's now enough evidence, "to support the conclusion that the risk of degenerative diseases from long-term exposure to space radiation may be of much greater concern than previously believed."

(3) Cancer risk

Space travel also brings cancer risk.

Another major area of concern is cancer.

Radiation exposure can cause genetic damage that may increase an astronaut's risk of developing cancer years after their mission.

Currently, NASA sets the radiation limit for astronauts at a 3 percent cancer fatality probability. For a mission on the ISS, where proximity to Earth provides some protection from radiation, women can stay about 18 months and men can stay about 24 months before exceeding the limit. But on a mission to Mars, astronauts would be way over the limit, according to Francis Cucinotta, Ph.D., a professor of health physics at University of

Nevada, Las Vegas, who authored the research on exposure limits. Cucinotta worked for NASA for more than a decade, and developed a database that tracks astronauts' exposure to radiation and cancer risk estimates. He told Health line it would be a question of ethics whether to raise the risk limit to allow astronauts to travel to Mars.

(4) Mental illness risk

But the hazards of space aren't the only risks astronauts face on a long voyage.

They also have to put up with each other, while maintaining their own sanity in a small, cramped space. The National Academies also examined NASA's evidence reports on mental health issues related to space travel and "behavioral health decrements" when team members aren't working well together.

Another report focused on the health risks associated with sleep loss, circadian rhythm issues, and work overload. Lastly, the committee reviewed evidence on risks related to "vestibular/sensorimotor alterations," which include issues like space motion sickness. Overall, the committee noted that all of NASA's reports were quite thorough, but recommended that NASA pay more attention to the interactions between different types of risks. For example, lack of sleep and being overworked could have a big impact on how well a team of astronauts works together. Teamwork issues are especially important to consider on long-duration missions, according to Neal.

"On a one- to two-week mission you are so busy, you don't have time for interpersonal issues to form," Neal told Health line. But on longer missions, more psychological factors come into play. She noted that being able to call family and friends back home and talk in real time has made a world of difference for astronauts' mental health and well-being.

But thosc immediate connections wouldn't be possible on a long mission to Mars — which could be a real source of stress for astronauts.

In conclusion, although, space travel is one kind of exciting and new travel entertainment activity, however, it can only let some rich people can enjoy the short time space travel journey. So, poor people won't enjoy this kind of travel entertainment. But, it also bring different risks when space travellers are catching the rocket to fly to the space anywhere to travel. Moreover, any space travellers have life danger when they are catching the rocket to fly to space anywhere to travel, even the cost is expensive, e.g. space travel facility, space travel destination entertainment arrangement.

They need spend too much money to build on the planet when the space travellers arrive the planet to travel. If the space travelling investor can not gain any reward to compensate their expenditure, then they will encounter much loss. Is it still worth to invest more than space exploration? Otherwise, if any space exploration is successful, then it may bring another earth existence in possible and human may attempt to live another planet in possible. So, it seems that space exploration can bring long term benefit more than space travel because space travel is one kind short time individual entertainment enjoyable benefit. Otherwise, space exploration is one kind long time human overall living benefit. It explains that why exploring space is more important than exploring space travel.

Mars exploration failure factors

What are Mars exploration possible failure factors? I shall indicate Mars exploration mission possible failure reasons as below:

On space exploration improvement aspect: US plans for the human exploration of Mars are best seen as a serious human spaceflight effort. It is possible that improvements in technologies will make flights to Mars feasible and survivable, but these technologies are still in development. Robotic exploration provides the scientific benefits to be gained from exploring Mars at lower cost and much lower risk. When these is a manned flights to Mars, serious political interest is lacking. A manned mission to Mars is not likely to occur for at least 10 years, if not longer.

The problem may include: How to provide fast speed space station transportation service between earth and Mars, less dangerous risk or high safety, providing more innovative space manned flight activities lead to space tourism or some other commercial activity involving human spaceflight. Acquiring earth observation satellites for security purposes, providing imagery, electronic intelligence and communications services, spacecraft, robotic and more advanced space shuttles, ability to maneuver in orbit, remain in space for long periods. So, space technology must need to be improved if space scientists hope to explore Mars to achieve to let human to live in possible in future one day.

On space science continue researching and development aspect: Why do space scientists need to continue space science research, if they hope to explore Mars more easily? Because we live in a society which depends on science and technology, those are very essentials seem undervalued perhaps because they are not understood. There are great concern in some quarter about the inadequacies and shortcomings in science funding, science education and the way space science in communicated to the public. For these questions example: Why do we need to choose Mars to live? How do we need explore Mars to live in success? What benefits and risks do we encounter in this Mars exploration process? So, space scientists have responsibilities to let pubic to know because they need people vote to support their Mars exploration mission. If people do not understand engine science , space science, medical science or whatever, then they are not equipped to get knowledgeably on science issues.

In space science, there are two main but not necessarily separate for spending, sometimes referred to collectively as research and development. Research is the acquisition of new knowledge. Development is the application of existing knowledge to new or improved user, such as exploration continue research of any new space exploration knowledge to Mars as well as they also need to learn how to apply existing Mars exploration knowledge to new or improved uses. However, there is no way of knowing where or when any kinds of new Mars exploration knowledge will find a practical application. But they need still continue to research and develop any possible new kinds of Mars exploration new technology.

However, researching and development is impossible without approval and funding. It is safe to say. Then, that some of the most vital work done, such as Mars exploration by space scientists is in preparing their funding applications. Also, space science is a around field, with a vary limited number of resources for cutting edge research. An idea for research and there is a fair chance that someone has already thought or it is already working on other similar earth seven planets , or other undiscovered researching planets which choice has higher successful chance to implement human living another earth mission. So, choice of which one space exploration mission is the best, it needs space scientists compare their benefits and risks in order to make final space exploration decisions.

On space exploration expenditure spending aspect: NASA needs to make budget for everything from launching missions to conducting educational programs, such as human space flight, which includes the shuttle and space station, gets around bit billion of that. Space missions are cheaper today than in earlier times, because the technology is in general cheaper and methods have been improved.

Billion dollar figures naturally keep a lot of people in work, and have an economic influence, but are there tangible returns that the ordinary citizen can consider over the entire range of space based activity, such as whether exploration of Mars mission is the most reasonable choice among other planet exploration choices? How will serious economic effect be influenced by this wrong failure space mission decision ?

One of the first and most obvious results of the space age was the rapid progress in satellite and communications technology, evident today is so many aspects of life that our interface with them is virtually seamless. What is the value of satellites? From weather reports, sports broad casts, and communication networks to geographic information systems, geophysical research and the global positioning system, we can earn the benefits of the space age every day of our lives. If nothing else had some of the space race, we would still have different reasons. In fact, that satellite technology has become a commercial enterprise means that it can pay its own way.

What do we get for our investment in space? The space environment offers conditions of microgravity, vacuum, and temperature extremes, which hold promise for experiments and possess not possible on earth. The vacuum of space , for example is better than the best vacuum attainable on earth. So , space scientists need to find methods how to flight this natural and dangerous space environment, it includes radiation, simulate, progress in developing more versatile , and efficient materials and engineering methods. However, these developments can bring indirect benefits to our space exploration development, such as computers, medical equipment and electronics science in general have all benefited from the space exploration development age.

However, space scientists need to make an analysis of the likely risks and benefits of any one space exploration research. There must be interested to know, for instance, how his/her idea would almost certainly to choose the planet living exploration, any planet living explorations must be at same stage , the come a point where the benefits outweigh the risks and the financial budget can be justified.

Deciding whether a risk is acceptable is necessarily subjective, such as the Mars exploration mission. Rocket testing is done in isolated areas, and launch paths or usually over wide stretches of ocean or sparsely populated land, when the rocket arrives the Mars land. It must need ensure safe and none crash or fire occurrence accident when the rocket arrives on the Mars land. Costly through a failure is the risks in unmanned missions are relatively strategic involving fire or pollution from rocket fuel , and falling space junk. Onboard radioactive substances can certainly give valid cause for concern, but once a craft has left earth orbit, the space men are out of danger, when their rocket arrives on the Mar's land.

By comparison with radio active,if you feel rocket fuel and space plane quickly, the risks do seem minimal probably, they are. We should put those possibilities into perspective, through, e.g. tens of thousands od people live in close proximity to airports, and face the prospect of having a burning airbus coming down coming down on top of them. It is something we live with, such as our solution concerns how to the Mars, when it only has one limit number of space station to let the rocket to land on Mars, and it can not cause any fire occurrence to bring life absolutely dangerous to our life, if we were living on the Mar's land one day. For instance, that microscopic organisms can survive and mutate in the microgravity and higher radiation levels of space stations.

What would happen if Mars people came back to Earth as passengers on an astronaut's clothing? Moreover, we must rightly consider the possibility of dangerous Martian microbes arriving on Earth in samples returned by robot explorer. Will quarantine conditions devised around known standard be sufficient? Suppose some of our own bacteria travel to Mars on our spacecraft survive on the surface, but mutate in the intense UV radiation. What kinds of diseases could they cause when human explorers arrive ?

In conclusion, mutant Earth bacteria will have to be dealt with of and when they are encountered. The possibility of native microbes from Mars arriving, though is already taken seriously enough by some people that an organization dedicated to seeing that samples are not returned is already in existence. Another problem is how adaptable living on Mars problem, how can human adapt to live in Mars in the silence of space environment , but it would be too much for modern city, light weight feeling when human does not need to walk on Mars' land. All of these issues will be human need to face problems, if space scientists can confirm Mars can be one adaptable planet to let us to live to compare other planets in the future possible one day.

- Space exploration possible
economic benefits

What are economic benefits of space exploration? Space exploration may bring these economic benefits as below: The critical drive of technological changes linked to the space industry. Firms may make technological leap that took billions in public funds to finance to carry on continue space exploration research continue in long term into the different kinds of space markets development, e.g. space resource exploration, space living environment exploration, space energy exploration , space tourism expenditure exploration etc.

For new entrants to all one space market, they may be assisted to invest to build their own rocket factories or space stations , how to design and rebuild reusable rockets easily when they anticipate to any kinds of space exploration activities. It can increase cooperation to develop future space exploration missions successful chance as well as expertise is increasingly consolidated within single firms, instead of across a multiplicity of vendors and contractors. Because any one space exploration activity, if there are many different countries' space exploration companies anticipate , it will bring more success in the process of designing, testing and improving products in all those space exploration companies in new and innovative ways.

Then, any one space exploration mission success, it also brings another or other new technological business chance. It helps to create monopolies or at least oligopoly and this provide sufficient incentive to innovate or drive down costs to US space industry sells its any space exploration products into international market as well as creating more space exploration manufacturing workers, space products salespeople, space science teacher etc. positions job opportunity to reduce unemployment ratio and encouraging more students choose space science subject to learn. It can change to the space exploration industry with long-term commercial, scientific and even military security, technical innovation economic benefits to global entrepreneurs, even when any one space exploration technological development reaches mature stage, then it will bring long term profits, as reducing cost and less risky businesses in possible.

In conclusion, it seems that space exploration industry may bring long term economic benefits more than long term economic loss. It depends on this factor whether how many space exploration technological firms can be encouraged to cooperate together. When any one space exploration activity/mission has many space exploration firms anticipation, then the space exploration activity/mission will have high successful chance. Otherwise, there are less number space exploration firms cooperate to carry on researching the space exploration activity/ mission, then it will have high failure chance. Some firms anticipative number will be one important influential factor to any one of space exploration activity/mission.

CHAPTER SIX

Computer tool useful leisure Consumer Behavior

Why China's computer manufacturing and product development industry will be global leader to compete US computer dominant market.

Nowadays, China's computer industry is the largetest hardware producer production and experts is dominated by Taiwanese firms. It is also the second largest personal computer (pc) market and domestic pc companies are top three sellers in global computer manufacturing and product development market. Forx example, Lenovo buys BM pc business in 2004 year. It implies US, IBM pc manufacturing leader can not dominate global computer market in possible in the future.

Reed Electronic Research, Yearbook Of World Electronic Data (2003) indicated that the leading computer producing countries of hardware production in US $millions and share share of total gogal production: The world region US was the global rank number one. In 1995 year, US had US $76,284 value, market value 26.5%. Then in 2000 year, US had increased up to US $ 90, 430 value, market share 24%. Till to 2003 year, US had fallen down to US $ 69,102 value, market share 21.7%. However, US hardware production was still the global rank number one , although its hardware production value had been falling down. But, the following second rank country, Japan and the third rank country, Singapore and the fourth rank country, Taiwan and the fifth rank county China which hardware production value could not exceed US till to 2003 year. However, although China had the lowest hardware production value US $5,600 to compare to among of these countries in 1995 year, but China had increased the value to US $65,000 and market share to 20.5%. Otherwise, Japan, Singapore and Taiwan value and market share had surprisingly fallen down below than

China value in 2003 year. Thus, it seemed that China will be a potential country to compete US hardware production industry after 2003 year.
Reed Electronic Research, Year book Of World Electronic Data (2003) also showed that these computer companies of China had these % of market share : Beijing Founder had 9.9%, Tsinghua Tongtang had 7.8%, dell had 7.2 % , IBM had 5.1% , HP had 4.8% of market share. Thus, it also seemed that China some computer companies will have impotant large market share percentage in global pc sale market. In the future, global hardware production and pc sale industry. China and Taiwan both countries will be one pc manufacturing and design and sale partner. The reason is that China and Taiwan had been the number one rank of markers of notebook pcs, motherboards, scanners, keyboards, add-on card optical drives, monitors and some network equipment etc. pc (personal computer) relative computer function products. It seems that these both countries had co-operated to research any computer relative products to sell to global computer market. They are also the original design manufacturers (DDMS) develop and manufacture over half the world's notebook pcs as well as their customers include all major branded pc vendors (OEMS).
Taiwan Minstry Of Economic Affairs (2003) indicated Taiwan's top notebook ODMS include: In 2003 year volume (thousands) Quanta had $8,500 sale volume thousands , for example, Quanta major OEM partners include Gateway, Dell, HP, IBM, Apple , Sharp, Sony, Fujitsu-Siemens (F/S). Compal had $6,000 sale volume (thousands) , Compal major OEM partners include Dell, HP, F/S, Toshiba, Acer. Thus, it also implied Taiwan had many small size and non famous brand of computer companies which choose to co-operate to be partners with some global large size and famous brand of computer companies to raise competitive effort in global computer market, such as Dell, IBM, HP, Gatway, Apple etc.
Thus, the future trend of computer new product manufacturing development will shift from US to Taiwan and SE Asia, then to China. However, what kind of knowledge work factors will be needed to China and Taiwan . In general, notebook manufacturing stages will include: The first process is design stage, it includes concept design, such as analyze need, create concept and set brand image as well as product planning, such as business case, specifications, industrial design and sourcing strategy. The second process is development stage, it includes design review steps, such as design review, such as mock-ups, electrical test as well as prototype build, such as commercial samples, integrated system test as well as pilot

production, such as production process design, pilot. Final process is production stage, it includes mass production, such as ramp-up, volume production, production testing and global distribution as well as sustaining support, such as speed bump, component replacement, technical support and warranty support. Thus, I believe that China and Taiwan must own thee knowledge work skillful of computer design and development professionals who can assist these two countries how to innovate their future computer development to change global traditional computer model to be renew and innovate computer model in the future.

Due to computer industry's stages of development and manufacturing are closely linked , need manufacturability , testing of sample products, concept design and product planning stay together in lead markets and branded vendors, design and development can be separated organizationally and geographically. Thus, China and Taiwan choose to co-operate to exchange their different skill, such as either China has own more concept design and product planning skill or more development skill or more production skill. Then, China will choose either one of the most beneficial comparative advantage among of them. To bring this one of the most beneficial co-operative advantage to attract Taiwan to choose either one of the beneficial comparative advantage of skill, such as either design or development or producton to already co-operate to compete the Western developed country US together.

Thus, US won't be the global computer industry development leader if both US country famous and large employee number computer companies, such as IBM and Apple which choose to outsource their pc design and development and production skill to China and Taiwan both countries to help them to develop global computer design and development and production skill to be upgraded. Thus, I feel these both countries will plan how to co-operate to compete US to win the global computer industry leader position in the future.

Factors influence consumers' laptop purchases.

In the future, instead of global computer manufacters need to consider the design, development and production processes, who also need to consider what factors can influence consumers' laptop purchases. Because any consumers have much different computer model and brand to choose to make final decision to buy any computers. If the computer manufacturer can predict what factors will be whose weakness(es) to influence global computer consumers to change whose mind or attitude to choose to buy other brands of computers, then it won't lose its many old computer customer numbers and reduces it market share in global computer market share.

Nowadays, in general computer has three kinds to provide to global consumers to choose to buy , such as laptop, notebook computers, desktops. it seems that laptop and notebook computers and desktops will have different factors to influence any consumers to choose to buy any brand of computer products. Thus, computer indsutry can divide three consumer groups, such as (stayers, satisfied switchers and dissatisfied switchers) of a computer company with respect to the factors influencing consumers' laptops or notebook computers or desktops purchases. However, I feel the factors can include such as core technicl features, post purchase services, prices and payment conditions, peripheral specification, physical appearance, value added features and connectivity and mobility seven main factors that are influencing consumers' laptop or notebook computer or desktop purchases in global computer industry market.

Ganesh et al., (2000) indicates the customer base of a company consists of three groups of consumers: stayers, satisfied switchers and dissatisfied switchers. Therefore, the consumers in this study replied to the question about whether the current brand that who were using was their first laptop brand or whether who had switched from a previous laptop brand. As a following question, consumers who had switched were asked to state the reason of why who switched from a previous laptop brand brand to their current brand. The options include overall dissatisfaction from the previous laptop brand and reasons other than dissatisfaction. Thus, computer companies need to know what factors influence either whose prior computer customers why who don't choose repeat to buy its any computer products or whose new potential computer customers why who don't choose to buy its any computer products in the first time choice. Thus, future computer manufacturers need to consider intangible salespeople service attitude or performance, such as salespeople current purchase and post purchase service, e.g. technical repair, model function explanation how to use the computer, instead of tangible product performance, e.g. computer appearance design , function , mobility and internet and document download speed connectivity function. Because salespeople and technicians' service performance can be represented to the computer image. If they can provide excellent service to let computer buyers to feel satisfactory, then they can help their computer company employer to build good image. So, staff service performance will be one important factor to influence computer consumers to make the final decision to choose to buy the brand of computer products more easily. Even, one famous brand computer company, such as IBM, Apple, Gateway, these any one of famous brand computer company must not attract any new (the first time) or repeat computer buyers to choose to buy their any kind of computer products , such as laptop, desktop or notebook more easily due to their famous brand. Althoug, these famous computer companies had built good image to let consumers have more confidence to buy any kind of their computer products. But, if these famous computer companies' salepeople or repair technicians can not provide excellent customer service or performance to satisfy their computer buyers' service need, e.g. explaining how to use the new computer, repair post purchase service etc. I believe these famous brands of computer consumers will not have more desire to prefer to chose to buy any one of these famous computer brand's products. Otherwise, if the other less famous computer companies' any kind of laptop, desktop or notebook sale price is higher than the famous brand of computer companies' products sale price, but their salepeople or technicians can provide more excellent service attitude or performance to satisfy their consumers' needs. It is possible that the new or first time computer buyers or repeat computer buyers will still choose to buy their computers. So, the famous or less famous computer brand is not one important factor to influence the computer buyer to decide either to buy the computer or not buy the computer. Otherwise, computer company's salepeople and repair technician whose service performance or attitude will be one important intangible factors to influence any first time (new) or repeat computer consumers to choose to buy any famous or less famous brand of computer company's product, instead of the tangible computer design appearance and reliable function and convenient mobility and long term durability etc. factors influences.

Can culture factor influence the computer consumer choice?

Durmza and Zengin, (2011:53) indicted marketers closely interested in this issue to know the family which changed and renewed in course in time. It provides an advantage for a marketer to know the family structure and its consumption characteristics. Nowadays, consumer behavior is influenced not only by consumer personalities and motivation, but also by the relationships within families. Family is a social group and it can be considered a crucial place in th perception of marketing (Durmaz, Yakup,

CELLK, Mucahit and ORUC, Reyhan, (2011).
The consumer buying behaviors examined through an empirical study. Then, it brings this question: Whether cultural factors will influnece the computer consumer choice. Choice and include computer brand choice, computer price choice, computer model choice, computer design choice, laptop or desktop or notebook product choice, new or second-hand old computer choice, the computer of manufacturing country choice, computer package choice etc. So, any consumer will consider to choose any one of these to decide to buy which kind of computer.
Every country computer consumers had different culture to influence their computer shopping choice. I feel culture can be explained how to influence to computer shopping such as: How do the country computer consumers buy and use their computer products habitually ? How do the country computer consumers react to th computer price changes, attractive advertising methods to satisfy whose needs and computer company store interiors? What underlying mechanisms operate to produce any one of the country computer consumers' responses? If computer marketers have answers to such these questions, who can make better managerial decisions how to adopt which computer target country (countries) consumers' culture.
Consumer behavior deals with many other issues, for instance (Priest, Carter and Statt, 2013: 19). How do we get information about products? How do we assess alternative products? How do different people choose or use different products? How do we decide on value for money ? How much risk do we take with what products? Who influences our buying decisions and our use of the product? How are brand loyalties formed and changed? For computer industry, it means that how computer consumers get information about computer products, how computer consumers assess alternative notebook, desktop, laptop computer products, how different age, country, culture, sex, student or working people or retired people computer consumers choose or use different kind of computer products, such as notebook, desktop, laptop computer products, how much risk computer consumers take with notebook, desktop, laptop computer products, the computer consumers' buying decisons and their use of the desktop or notebook or laptop computer products will be influenced by whom, e.g. family, friends, teacher, employer, computer salepeople, advertisement marketer etc. , computer company brands how are formed and changed by whom, e.g. computer consumers, computer company competitors,

marketers, different countries' culture etc.

Durmaz and Jablonski, (2012:56) also explained culture is the essential character of a society that distinguishes it from other cultural groups. The underlying elements of every culture are the values, language, myths, customs, laws and the artifacts or products that are transmitted from one generation to the next (Lamb, Hair and Deniel, 2011: 371). Culture is the most fundamental determinant of a person's wants and behavior. Whereas, lower creatives are governed by instinct, human behavior is largely learned. The child growing up in a society leans a basic set of values, perceptions, preferences and behaviors through a process of socialization involving the family and other social roles. So, I feel different country have different culture to influence as well as different country computer consumers who have different computer purchase and consume habitually. So, computer manufacturers ought focus on manufacturing the unique need and characteristics to satisfy any country's consumers' needs.

What is my idea about future global computer competition and factors influence computer consumer behavior ?

In conclusion, future computer industry development will trend that computer manufacturers need to consider every country's computer comsumer culture. Because every country computer consumers who will have different computer consumption habitually if who can predict what the country most computer consumers culture, then they can have more confidence to sell their computers to different country markets. Moreover, US computer manufacturers need to consider China and Taiwan computer manufacturing technology because it is possible that these both countries will be its main competitor among different computer manufacuring countries. Because thess both countries will cooperate to research new model of different computers to attract global computer consumers to choose to buy their new model of computer products in the future. Finally, computer manufacturers need to consider salepspeople and repair technicians service performance because computer consumers will consider intangible service performance , instead of tangible computer quality and price and style etc. factors . The main reason is that any computer have chance to be needed to repair and salespeople' skill will influence the computer consumer to make final decision to choose to buy the brand of computer. Thus, these factors will influence global computer development and trend in the future.

- Computer industry related service market development

What kinds of technologies innovation products will impact our future lives.

Europe in the 21 St Century is a technological society, how today technological trends could impact upon society in ways to be fully considered by clients' needs. What technological advancement products which can carry trend with it the promise of saving time, or assisting business or manufacturer industry clients to do more in the same amount of time.

In our clients buying choice view point, who ought hope any technological innovation products which can offer them that the opportunity to do things more efficiently. I shall suppose that technological innovation will be the main factor which can attract future many clients' purchase choice from the owned technological innovation product seller. For example, mobility, resource security , electronic government technological innovation products will be popular trend in future technological innovation product market.

- Autonomous automatic vehicle

Can autonomous vehicles be popular in the future driving market? Will your child soon be driving you to work? The autonomous vehicles (artificial intelligent vehicles) will change the responsible driver concept. Why does autonomous vehicles will be future popular driving tools?

In fact, autonomous vehicles have these feature characteristics to differ to compare our common traditional driving tools. Their characteristics, such as real-time human control option, advantage of the large amount of high -quality mapping data of possesses to programing travel routes, exploring ways in which autonomous vehicle technology can be integrated with existing parking infrastructure to produce " driverless parking systems" accessible via existing personal electronic devices, e.g. smartphones is demonstrating the use of fully automated road transport systems in Europe and developing guidelines to design and implement such systems.

With some analysts predicting that by 2022 year , there will be around 1.8 billion automotive machine -to-machine connection its is clear that a large amount of data will be generated by vehicle in the future. Thus, this level of communication between automated vehicles should make to possible for such vehicles to navigate to destinations and interact with other vehicles and objects most effectively than a human brain. Moreover, they believe the chance of automatic vehicles' highway accidents occurrence will be less than traditional human driving vehicles.

Thus, the increased connectivity required to facilitate automation of vehicles would significantly improve the degree of monitoring of the performance of such vehicles. Individual owners would be able to better maintain and enhance their vehicles with improvements in fuel efficiency and lesser fuel spending and safety. This could also provide further benefits, such as terms of reducing traffic jams, reduced pedestrian exposure to pollution and lower risk of road-traffic and pedestrian incidents occurring, particularly in urban areas.

The rise of autonomous vehicles is also likely to combine with continuing electrification of vehicles as telecommunications software and hardware and further integrated into vehicles. Thus, the rental-orientated and purchase-orientated automatic vehicle business both models will have chance to be raised in future global driving market.

It causes the responsibility tends to lie with human drivers of vehicles will be decreased. A new set of IT skills in addition to a practical ability to drive and operate a more digital type of driving machine as well as it might impact upon existing vehicle users in terms of requiring re-training, particularly those less able to learn. Even, future public transport will have possible to be changed from non-human driving and change to automatic vehicle market will be individual and business both client markets in possible.

In conclusion, to success to sell non manual driving tools. The non manual driving sellers need to know how to solve these two artificial intelligent vehicles innovation questions: Could our future living habits change as a direct segment of changing transport behaviors? Will autonomous transport simply become and essential transportation tools for our homes and workplaces? Thus, if manufacturers want artificial intelligent vehicles sale number increases, which needs to influence future whose clients to accept this kind of non -human driving tools can be satisfy to change their traditional driving living habits for their new habit of non -manual driving method to substitute traditional manual driving tools.

● 3 D printer

Can 3 D printer be popular sale to manufacturing industry clients? What could be the effects to the physical environment and human health of such application 3D printer to copy to manufacture any productions? For example, medical equipment products, car keys, guns, furniture etc. different heavy or light weight manufacturing products.

The benefits to 3 D printer include: less production time, reducing purchase bulk or materials to produce any products, reducing to employ worker number to produce products, workers can learn to use 3D printer to copy to manufacture any products easily, to avoid air or water pollution to pollute working environment to influence worker health and safe production in factories, employers can pay less wages to employ less workers, workers can also raise more efficient during using 3 D printers to manufacture any products.

Thus, in the future 3 D printers can be popular to be used to copy to manufacture for these any products, e.g. jewelry or weapon industry products. In fact, 3 D printer is an additive manufacturing technology for making three- dimensional object, of almost one sharp using a digital model. Such as jewelry manufacturers apply it to copy to manufacture new kind of jewelry, hospitals can apply it to copy to manufacture any new medical equipment, weapon manufacturers can apply it to copy to manufacture any new gun weapons, aerospace or air plan manufacturers can apply it to manufacture new air plane engineering equipment or space exploration equipment or transportation tools. Thus, 3 D printer application will be popular to different aspects of manufacturing industry.

Future expected impacts and development for 3 D printer development. A macro economy level impact of 3 D printing will be considered to manufacturing industry business consumer-based economy and the societal behavioral acceptance in factories and offices manufacturing environment.

However, buying habits as individuals are able to print their own products, in comfort of their own home. Activity would be changed from traditional shopping methods to purchase 3 D printer to copy to manufacture own same products at home. Consumers can also choose how to design to print the product, rather than the manufacturing process itself is what consumers will be paying for and thus these is the potential for a design -lead choice behavior. Manufacturers don't need to buy many materials to manufacture products, they can use 3D printer , such as individual manufacturing machine parts, which could drastically improve their ability to design and manufacture more effective machine and components.

In conclusion, how to sell 3 d printer successfully. 3 D printer sellers need to know what advantages can give to 3 D individual consumption buyer and business buyer to let them to know to aim to let them to accept to change their buying behavior and manufacturing behavior for some products. There are some questions for consumers to attempt to answers:

What will the implications be the level of personal interactions between individuals in society of all of our products were to be manufacturing at home?

How would this change our typical buying habits and what would be the impact on our economy?

Would an increased use of 3D printing technology in the home or factory accelerate this process and what would be the implications for local high streets?

Would economies change being-focused will digital design skills having a greater benefits than traditional manufacturing methods?

If the ability to print everyday items at home becomes a reality , who is society would have the greatest access to such technology?

If a particular demographic section (age, gender, race, income levels can be in factor to influence 3D printer consumer group, e.g. the 3 D printer buyer needs skills to manufacture any products, it seems only represented in a younger demographic. Could this mean that older members of society would not be able to benefit from 3 d printed projects?

In micro economy view point, although 3 D printer has benefits to individual and manufacturing consumers to reduce that their shopping or manufacturing expenditure, more design choice, raising worker individual skill and work performance. However, in macro economy view point, it also bring disadvantages to society. For example, if some members of society could not work move quickly, as a result than others, then what might be the impact upon their employability , e.g. causing unemployment of the 3D printer skillful learners who can not upgrade their working skill. Then, their employers will choose to dismiss these low skillful level 3 D printing learning skillful workers. Consequently, it will cause these member group of worker unemployment in the future society in possible. In conclusion, employers can not neglect how to train workers to learn how to apply 3 D printing skills to copy to manufacture any products.

- Massive open online course education

Will online education change traditional education? Basically, the students who choose to study from online channel, who must need have personal computers at home or school and often use internet from online platforms. In contrast to traditional methods of teaching with much small class size because every student can learn from online course at home. It means one teacher can choose to teach only one student from online channel. So, the teacher can stay at home or school as well as the student can stay at home , both of them can teach and learn from online teaching platform at the same time.

Whether the primary school, high school and university students who can accept to choose their learning habit to learn from this kind of online learning method more easily. In fact, online education will resultant impact on any teaching competitiveness. Due to , it is attempted to develop one kind of new technological education method to replace the traditional classroom by face -to-face teaching method between teacher and students contact.

However, it is not all course are suitable to adopt online teaching method and some courses re pointedly directed towards areas of interest that help education providers to also sell other online course products what other simply promote passive learning. For example, music, art, history, math, commerce courses which can be taught by teacher from online channel more easily. Because they do not need students to go to laboratory to do any experiments. Otherwise, engineering, food science, space science, medicine , doctor courses which need students go to laboratory to do experiments often. Thus, they are not suitable to be taught by teacher from online channel. Classroom teaching is more suitable to them.

Although, online teaching is low cost , due to that schools do not need many classrooms, even employ many teachers. So, they only buy computers and provide online education and less teachers are employed to teach whose students. So, it brings this question: Simply coursing cost barriers of success to education would not necessarily result in automatic take-up by young student consumers. May also need to think about best to education market, particularly to disadvantaged groups , such as older generations with lower computer and internet skills.

Who would be the winners and losers of an education market based upon such stronger principles of knowledge sharing and how can the institutions employing the use of such online or classroom or distance learning education methods be appropriately supported to maintain the high quality of further education? It seems to persuade students to choose online learning, the only method is that to let students feel online education can provide higher teaching quality level to compare traditional classroom learning method.

Other potential impacts of education market method relates more to education going online and a shift away from the more traditional forms of campus-based teaching in highest education . Would improving access to online education have the effect of increasing online students number. Due to who accept to choose online learning from traditional classroom learning habits . Thus, this is one learning habit change challenge for the traditional classroom learning students to adopt the online learning habit change.

In conclusion, for online education providers who need to consider how to change traditional classroom learning and teaching habit to adapt new online learning and teaching habit, as well as how to provide online teaching quality is higher level to compare to traditional teaching quality if who want their online education service businesses are successful.

www.ingramcontent.com/pod-product-compliance
Ingram Content Group UK Ltd.
Pitfield, Milton Keynes, MK11 3LW, UK
UKHW041641190726
13854UKWH00006B/2638